Resources for Teaching English: 14–16

Also available from Continuum

Resources for Teaching Mathematics: 14–16, Colin Foster
Resources for Teaching Shakespeare: 11–16, Fred Sedgwick
Resources for Teaching Creative Writing, Johnnie Young

RESOURCES FOR TEACHING ENGLISH: 14–16

David A. Hill

continuum

Teachers' resources to accompany this book are available online at:
http://education.hill.continuumbooks.com
Please visit the link and register with us to receive your password and to access these downloadable resources.
If you experience any problems accessing the resources, please contact Continuum at:
info@continuumbooks.com

Continuum International Publishing Group

The Tower Building	80 Maiden Lane
11 York Road	Suite 704
London	New York
SE1 7NX	NY 10038

www.continuumbooks.com

As this book was going to press a new coalition government was making changes within education, so references to the TDA, QCDA and any other governmental website may no longer be completely up-to-date.

British Library Cataloguing-in-Publication Data
A catalogue record for this book is available from the British Library.

ISBN: 9780826421005 (paperback)

Library of Congress Cataloging-in-Publication Data
Hill, David A.
Resources for teaching English 14-16 / David A. Hill.
    p. cm.
  ISBN 978-0-8264-2100-5 (pbk.)
  1. English language and literature—Study and teaching (Secondary). 2. Language arts (Secondary). I. Title.

LB1631.H497 2010   428.0071'2—dc22

Typeset by Pindar NZ, Auckland, New Zealand
Printed and bound in Great Britain by Bell & Bain Ltd, Glasgow.

Contents

Introduction

The object of *Resources for English 14–16* is to provide KS4 teachers of English with a wealth of ready-made lessons that will make lesson preparation easier. The book contains a set of 70 different lesson plans, each with a related photocopiable task sheet. These are thematically arranged across eight different topics, with between seven and 11 lesson plans/task sheets for each topic. The majority of the lesson plans are text-based, that is, there is a reading passage for them. Just over half of these texts are examples of poetry, mostly contemporary; the rest are various kinds of prose: short story, novel extracts, magazine articles and essays. The texts are worked into through a range of typically student-centred brainstorming activities, and then worked out of with activities on analysing form and language, and through writing and drama activities. Classics are also included, with work by Dickens, Blake, Wordsworth and Browning, and modern classics feature poetry by the likes of Carol Ann Duffy, Simon Armitage, Peter Porter, Brian Patten and U. A. Fanthorpe. The activities presented work rigorously around the criteria laid down in the National Curriculum Programme of Study for KS4, and these are referenced on the Continuum website for this book (http://education.hill.continuumbooks.com). Over the 70 lesson plans, there is complete coverage of all the criteria. However, this collection of lesson plans also has its eye on the future, and the intention to integrate English language and literature study, hence the text-based approach.

The lesson plans represent 'a way' of working; each teacher will adapt these plans to suit his or her needs, as there is no one recipe for every class; I hope, however, that what is presented here will provide a useful lesson base. I should add that, because of the space available, the notes on the texts are far from exhaustive; I have tended to go for the central features of the texts, relating to both content and structure. There is always more for you and the students to explore. Most of the texts are available online, and the relevant sites are referenced in each lesson plan; texts that are not available online are provided in the Resource Bank at the back of the collection. Additional useful websites are also listed on the Continuum website for this book, for example YouTube links where performances of poems can be watched and readings can be listened to. I hope, dear colleagues, that you have as much fun teaching these lessons as I did researching, writing and trialling them.

David A. Hill
Budapest
March, 2010

Section 1   The World of School

Memories of junior school

Introduction: Through the Carol Ann Duffy poem 'In Mrs Tilscher's Class' students explore their own memories of primary school and the way that people remember their past in general.

Aims and outcomes
- To read and discuss how a writer makes a place come alive
- To explore and write about their own memories of a place

Resources required: The poem 'In Mrs Tilscher's Class' from Carol Ann Duffy (1990) *The Other Country*. London: Anvil Press Poetry. You can find it online at:

 www.tusitala.org.uk/blog/blog.php?bid=303

Lesson starter (5 minutes): Ask the students to write down the name of the teacher they had in their final year at junior school. Ask them to briefly note some of the things they remember about lessons with that teacher, about the classroom, about their classmates, and any specific events they recall.

Main lesson (40 minutes)
- Put the students into groups of four to talk about their memories. Elicit what sort of things they remembered and note them on the board – categorize them as you list them under headings:
  Teacher/Classroom/Pupils/Events/Lessons/Playground and any other categories that arise.
- If elements such as particular sounds, smells and tastes haven't arisen already, ask which ones come into mind when they think of that class or the school in general, and list them under Senses.
- Ask the students how they felt in their final year at junior school. If necessary, prompt with questions: were you sad that you were leaving? Was junior school a happy time for you?
- Give out copies of the poem (or show it on the interactive whiteboard) and ask them to read it individually.
- Ask them if there is anything they don't understand in the poem and gloss that. Two cultural points they may be unfamiliar with are:
  a) Brady and Hindley and the so-called 'Moors Murders' in 1963–65, when Ian Brady and Myra Hindley sexually abused and killed five children.
  b) 'A skittle of milk' refers to the one third pint of milk every child had at morning break 1946–70.
- Give them the task sheet and ask them to do Activity 1 (list the things they find in the poem in the appropriate column) individually, then compare with a partner. Call back answers from the whole class, and add them under the class's list on the board. Ask them to spot any similarities between what they remembered and what Duffy writes about. Also any major differences, and what the reasons may be for that.
- Ask the students which features of Duffy's poem they can relate to and why. (e.g. 'I can relate to *chalky pyramids rubbed to dust* because I was board monitor in the class a few times, and I remember rubbing out what the teacher had written.')
- Ask the students to do Activity 2 on the task sheet individually, then discuss their answers with a partner. Call back the answers from the whole class.
- Ask the students to work through Activity 3 individually and discuss their answers with a partner. Call back the answers from the whole class.

(continued on page 4)

TASK SHEET: **Memories of junior school**

1. Read the poem 'In Mrs Tilscher's Class' and complete the table below with words and short phrases related to the topics in the headings.

Teacher	Pupils	Classroom	Lessons	Events	Playground	Senses
Mrs Tilscher	A dunce	Chalky				

2. Look at the second verse of the poem. What does this tell you about the writer's feelings about being in Mrs Tilscher's class? What images help give the impression, and what effect does being at school have on her?

3. Think about the figures of speech used in the poem.
   a) What figure of speech is 'the classroom glowed like a sweet shop'?

   b) What is the effect of it?

   c) Find another example of the same figure of speech and write it below.

   d) What is the effect of this one?

   e) What figure of speech is the 'laugh of a bell'?

   f) What is the effect of it?

   g) Find another example of the same figure of speech and write it below.

   h) What is the effect of it?

4. Reread the poem from 'A rough boy . . .' to the end. What is the relationship between what the boy, what the writer asked Mrs Tilscher and the general feeling behind the whole last verse? Write some sentences to explain this.

5. Is the poet successful at describing her feelings at that time? Why/why not?

- Ask the students to do Activity 4 individually, then exchange their writing with a partner for comparison and comment. Discuss their answers in a whole-class setting.
- Ask the students to discuss Activity 5 in pairs and tell another pair what they think.

Plenary (15 minutes)
- Round the lesson up with a discussion of individual feelings about the poem and its success.
- Discuss the poem as a 'poem' – it's form (irregular verses, no rhyme or chime, irregular syllable patterning) and language use.

Homework: Ask the students to write a poem or a paragraph of prose about their memories of their final junior school teacher's class.

Differentiation (of homework product): Students who don't want to/can't write about their final junior school class memories, might be offered a variety of alternatives:
- Memories of another junior school class
- Memories of somewhere they went, for example on holiday at a camp site: the tent, the people, the events, and so on.
- Memories of a place they used to go to regularly when they were younger, e.g. a sports or other club, cubs or brownies.

Learning more than classroom subjects

Introduction: Through the comparison of two similarly-titled poems the students will explore the wider lessons of life they learn through other events that occur at school.

Aims and outcomes

- Discovering meaning through guided close reading and discussion in groups
- Dealing with the formal structure of a poem and the effect it creates
- Writing a personal response to a piece of literature

Resources required: The poems 'The Lesson' from David A. Hill (1986) *The Eagles and the Sun.* Niš: Prosveta (Resource Bank) and 'The Lesson' from Edward Lucie-Smith (1961) *A Tropical Childhood and Other Poems.* Oxford: Oxford University Press. This second poem is available online at:

 www.guardian.co.uk/books/2007/jul/27/poetry.featuresreviews
http://thekumarexperience.wordpress.com/2009/02/21/poetry-the-lesson-by-edward-lucie-smith

The Lucie-Smith poem has also been anthologized in: Donachy M (Ed.) (2007*) 101 Poems about Childhood.* London: Faber.

Lesson starter (5 minutes): Ask the students to think about something specific they have learnt at school in a particular subject area recently. Call back some examples from the whole class.

Main lesson (50 minutes)

- Ask the students to do Activity 1 on the task sheet. Once they have thought of something, they can discuss their ideas in pairs. Then call back suggestions and list them on the board.
- Give half the class Poem A (Hill) and the other half Poem B (Lucie-Smith). Ask them to read their poem, think about the questions on the task sheet individually, then discuss it in groups of three or four with others who have read the same poem.
- Put the students together in pairs (or pairs of pairs) who have read a different poem. Ask them to complete Activity 3 on the task sheet. Give copies of the other poem to all students.
- Make a table as in task sheet Activity 3 on the board; call back suggestions from the whole class and write them up. Generate discussion about the answers you get.
- Activity 4: Ask all the students to look at Poem B (Lucie-Smith) and work out the formal structure of it ((a) 2 verses in (b) ABCBDADC rhyme-scheme, with (c) ten-foot lines).
- Activity 5: Ask the students to look at Poem A (Hill) and examine the punctuation (brackets/ single apostrophes for thoughts; speech marks for words said), and the effect of the words used in lines 11–14 (all single-syllable words, except for *silent* and *upon*, both of which are 'soft' sounds, reflecting the 'stillness' after the teacher's death; also the assonance (*all- awe*) and consonance (*still-all, we-were*) are all soft 'deadening' sounds adds to this effect).

Plenary (5 minutes): Engage the whole class in a discussion about which of the two poems they prefer and saying why.

Homework: Ask the students to complete Activity 6 on the task sheet for homework, using the ideas discussed in the Plenary discussion.

Differentiation: When the students discuss their own 'other learning', make room for a different range of experiences and where there may have been racial issues, bullying and different experiences between girls and boys. Try to ensure that a broad range of experiences are talked about and noted.

Learning more than classroom subjects

1. You learn many things at school. Perhaps you have recently learnt how to do differential calculus in maths, or about rubber production in Indonesia in geography. But you also learn other lessons related to areas such as relationships and social behaviour. Think of some things like these that you have learnt in the last year or two.

2. Read the poem you are given and think about these things:
   a) Whose voice do you hear speaking?
   b) What is the important event that happens?
   c) How does the speaker feel about school?
   d) What is the *lesson* that the speaker learns?
   When your teacher tells you, discuss your ideas with others who have read the same poem as you.

3. Work with someone who has read the other poem. Tell each other about your poem, then make notes about the similarities and differences in the two poems.

	Poem A (Hill)	Poem B (Lucie-Smith)
Which places in the school does the action take place?		
What similar event triggers the poem?		
What emotions does the speaker have about what happens?		
What is the *lesson* that is learnt?		

4. Read Poem B (Lucie-Smith). It is organized very formally. What are the three key elements of its structure? Write them below:
   a) Verse organization :

   b) Rhyme scheme:

   c) Line length:

5. Read Poem A (Hill). It has a blank verse form, but has some noticeable effects related to the punctuation, and the words used in lines 11–14. Examine these and discuss them with a partner.

6. Write a paragraph saying which of the two poems you prefer and why.

Tensions at secondary school

Introduction: This extract comes from *To Sir, With Love* by E. R. Braithwaite (New York: Jove, 1959) which tells the story of a black West Indian teacher – Rick Braithwaite – teaching in a rough working-class secondary school in London's East End in the 1950s.

Main aims and outcomes
- To enhance cross-cultural understanding and critical thinking
- To offer two different writing activities, one involving personal opinion related to the content of the text, the other to transform a text into another narrator's standpoint
- To give opportunity for drama work and the critical assessment of performance

Resources required: The appropriate section from Chapter 14 of the novel (Resource Bank).

Lesson starter (10 minutes): Ask the students what they know about immigration into the UK after World War II. Discuss what the situation was like for the first West Indians and Asians who moved to Britain (prejudice, difficulties in finding housing, only menial jobs available, etc.).

Main lesson (40 minutes)
- Explain that the students are going to read an extract from the novel *To Sir, With Love* about a West Indian engineer from British Guiana (now Guyana) who works as a teacher in a secondary school on London's East End. Students there leave school at 14, and he starts a teaching system based on respect: boys call girls Miss + surname, girls call boys by their surnames. The scene takes place at breaktime, while Braithwaite is helping some of the boys to lace up a football, and Pamela Dare is the only girl present.
- Ask the students to do Activity 1 on the task sheet individually, then discuss their ideas in a group of four. Call back suggestions and note them on the board in three columns: students', colleagues' and wider school community reactions.
- Activity 2. Students read and answer individually, then discuss their ideas with a partner. Call back answers from the whole class.
- Ask the students who they think the protagonist is in this extract (Pamela Dare). Ask them to reread the extract and do Activity 3, noting down up to six words and phrases that are used to describe her. Call their answers back and note them on the board. Ask what the effect of this is (to portray her as a strong, forceful and dominant character, more mature than the boys)
- Activity 4. Students think about their answers in relation to the extract and their own opinions. Ask them to discuss their ideas in a group, then open it up as a whole class discussion.
- Activity 5. Students explore their feelings about what is said, and differences between the 1950s and now. Ask them to swap and discuss their writing. Start a class discussion.
- In Activity 6 the students act out the scene in sevens. With uneven classes, one student can be the narrator, while the others 'walk through' the actions and say their lines. Otherwise, you or a student could narrate while the groups act the scene out simultaneously.

Plenary (10 minutes): Have the groups perform their version for the others, and then have a class discussion on which was the most successful interpretation and why.

Homework: Ask what point of view the event is written from (the teacher's). Ask the students to choose either Denham, Potter or Pamela Dare and to write the extract seen from that character's point of view, with them as first-person narrator.

Differentiation: The whole activity is about racial differentiation (West Indian/white British), male/female student differentiation, role differentiation (teacher-student) and time differentiation (the 1950s to now) and the activities suggested explore these areas.

TASK SHEET: Tensions at secondary school

1. The story of *To Sir, With Love* (E. R. Braithwaite, 1959) is about how a young West Indian engineer gets a job teaching in a secondary school in the East End of London in the 1950s. What problems do you think he faced? Note down some ideas.

2. Read the extract and answer the following questions:
   a) What happens to start the whole event in this scene?

   b) How do you understand Potter's first comment? How else can it be understood? What did Potter intend?

   c) What role does Pamela Dare take in relation to the teacher?

   d) What makes her comments so successful with her classmates?

   e) Why does she also attack Seales?

3. Look at the language that the author uses to describe Pamela Dare in this scene. Write down some of the phrases used below. What effect does this have?

4. Potter says 'I was only having a little joke and Sir didn't mind'. Do you think the teacher really didn't mind? Do you think it is an acceptable remark for a student to make to a teacher? How far do you think that what Seales says in his penultimate speech is true?

5. Do you think things happen and are said in this extract that might have been acceptable in Britain in the 1950s, but which would not be acceptable in your school now? Write a paragraph explaining your ideas.

6. Get together in a group of seven and take one of the roles each (Braithwaite, Denham, Fernman, Seales, Potter, Tich Jackson, Pamela Dare). You are going to act out the scene. Decide how you will stage it, and set up part of the classroom accordingly, then practise it through a couple of times.

Playing with the language of school

Introduction: The students will read an extract from *The Mock Turtle's Story* – a chapter from Lewis Carroll's classic children's novel *Alice's Adventures in Wonderland*. It is hoped that many students will be familiar with the book, either from reading it when younger or seeing a staged or film version.

Aims and outcomes

- To read and enjoy an amusing piece of English
- To understand the way that English plays with words (homophones, homographs)
- To enable students to create their own puns and use them successfully in their own production

Resources required: A copy of 'The Mock Turtle's Story', beginning at '"When we were little," the Mock Turtle went on at last . . .' down to '"Tell her something about the games now."' It is online at:

 www.literature.org/authors/carroll-lewis/alices-adventures-in-wonderland

(click on Chapter 9 'The Mock Turtle's Story' and scroll down to the correct section.)

Lesson starter (5 minutes): Ask the students if they know who Lewis Carroll was – elicit titles of books, poems and any other information. You might reasonably expect *Alice's Adventures in Wonderland, Through the Looking-Glass, and What Alice Found There,* the long poem 'The Hunting of the Snark', and individual poems from the two *Alice* stories, such as 'Jabberwocky' and 'You Are Old Father William'.

Main lesson (45 minutes)

- Give out the task sheet and ask students to work in pairs to complete Activity 1. Elicit answers from around the class.
- Ask the students to do Activity 2 individually; decide if it needs to be a dictionary activity or not. Possible answers: *A pun is a joke that depends on playing with words, and which exploits the ambiguity between similar sounding words.* There are two ways in which puns work: through homographs – *words which are spelt the same but have different meanings* (e.g. *can* = to be able; *can* = metal container), and through homophones – *words which sound the same but are written differently* (e.g. *eight – ate; bear – bare*).
- Elicit examples of homophones and homographs that students have found.
- Ask students to do Activity 3 in pairs; elicit their answers in a whole-class setting. (a) works because *tune a* (meaning to make an instrument sound right) sounds like *tuna* (the fish), and the effect is added to by the homograph *bass* which is a type of fish and a type of instrument (although the pronunciation is different). (b) works because the verb *flies* and the noun *flies* are written and said in the same way. (c) works because the noun *pupils* means both students and part of the eye.
- Give out the extract from 'The Mock Turtle's Story' and ask students to do Activity 4. When they have finished, elicit their answers – you might want to write them on the board.
- Ask them to complete the table in Activity 5 based on the previous discussion. Answers:

(continued on page 12)

TASK SHEET: Playing with the language of school

1. In the extract from *Alice's Adventures in Wonderland* which you are going to read, the Mock Turtle is telling Alice about his school days, aided by his friend the Gryphon. Tell a partner what other episodes you know from either of Lewis Carroll's two books, *Alice's Adventures in Wonderland* and *Through the Looking-Glass, and What Alice Found There.*

2. Look at the three words below. If necessary, use a dictionary to find out what they mean, and write a definition of each, and some examples of (b) and (c).

   a) A pun is _____

   b) A homophone is _____
      These are some examples: 1) _____ and _____; 2) _____
      and _____; 3 _____ and _____.

   c) A homograph is _____

      Some examples are 1) _____ meaning _____ and also
      meaning _____; 2 _____ meaning _____ and also
      meaning _____; 3 _____ meaning _____ and also
      meaning _____.

3. Look at these puns:
   a) You can tune a guitar, but you can't tuna fish. Unless, of course, you play bass. (Douglas Adams)
   b) Time flies like an arrow. Fruit flies like a banana.
   c) Did you hear about the cross-eyed teacher who couldn't control his pupils?
      Talk about them with a partner and discuss what makes them work.

4. Read the extract from *Alice's Adventures in Wonderland*. As you read, underline all the puns that you find, then compare with a partner.

5. Write the words that Lewis Carroll was punning on in the table below.

Mock Turtle's Word	Punning on . . .	Mock Turtle's Word	Punning on . . .
Tortoise	*taught us*	Seaography	
Reeling		Drawling	
Writhing		Stretc.hing	
Ambition		Fainting in Coils	
Distraction		an old crab	
Uglification		Laughing	
Derision		Grief	
Mystery		Lessons	

6. All of these puns use homophones, except one, which is a homograph. Which is the homograph?

7. Find two or three puns (or make some up) and tell your friends. Do they think they are funny? How do they work?

Mock Turtle's Word	Punning on . . .	Mock Turtle's Word	Punning on . . .
Tortoise	*Taught us*	Seaography	*Geography*
Reeling	*Reading*	Drawling	*Drawing*
Writhing	*Writing*	Stretc.hing	*Sketc.hing*
Ambition	*Addition*	Fainting in Coils	*Painting in oils*
Distraction	*Subtraction*	an old crab	*Crab = bad-tempered*
Uglification	*Multiplication*	Laughing	*Latin*
Derision	*Division*	Grief	*Greek*
Mystery	*History*	Lessons	*Lessons*

- Elicit the answer to Activity 6. *Crab* – meaning the sea creature and a bad-tempered person – we use the adjective *crabby* still in contemporary English, rather than say someone is *a crab*.
- Ask students to do Activity 7. They can then share the puns they think of in groups of four.

Plenary (10 minutes)
- Elicit some of the puns they have come up with from the whole class, and discuss how they work.

Homework: Ask students to find more examples of puns, say a minimum of two which work through homographs and two which work through homophones.

Differentiation
- You will need to make allowances for students who do not have *Alice* as an automatic piece of cultural baggage.
- You might do this by getting those who know to tell some of the story, or by showing extracts from one of the five film versions (Directors: Norman Z. Mcleod, 1933; Dallas Bower, 1950; Disney, 1951 (cartoon); William Sterling, 1972; Tim Burton, 2010).

Passing exams

Introduction: Through the Brian Patten poem 'The Minister for Exams' students will explore their attitudes to exams and also the position of the exam setters.

Aims and outcomes

- To explore and discuss attitudes to and feelings about exams
- To read, enjoy and analyse a contemporary poem

Resources required: The poem 'The Minister for Exams' from Brain Patten (1996) *Armada.* London: Flamingo, or online at:

 www.spikemagazine.com/pattenminister.php

or from:

 www.poetryarchive.org/childrensarchive/singlepoem.do?poemId=5921

where there is also a recording of Brian Patten reading the poem.

Lesson starter (10 minutes): Start the lesson as if you are going to give the students a test. Have enough A4 paper for each student to have a piece, and say something like: 'Right class . . . take everything off your desks except for a pen. I'm coming round to give you a piece of paper. When you get it, put your name and class at the top and today's date. We're going to have a test.' Go through with the whole 'game' seriously and in full 'teacher testing mode' until they all have paper and are sitting facing front. Then say 'Now, no talking or copying. First question . . .' Then pause, and say: 'How did you feel about this? Write down some words, phrases, sentences about your feelings and emotions when you knew you were going to have a test.' Give them time to write, individually. Then ask them to confer in groups of four; elicit ideas from the whole class. You might note some of the things they say on the board.

Main lesson (40 minutes)

- Give out the task sheet and ask them to read and answer the questions in Activity 1 individually; then group them in fours to discuss their ideas. Call back answers from the whole class.
- Ask them to do Activity 2 individually. They should write their answers on the sheet of paper you gave them. It is import that they don't talk or discuss their ideas at this stage. Do it like a test. You can give them a time limit – 15 minutes, telling them the time each 3 minutes.
- Ask them to get into the same group of four to discuss their answers. You can ask them to decide who they think got the answers right. When they have finished, call back some answers from around the class and ask other to comment on them.
- Ask them to stay in their fours and do Activity 4. Discuss their ideas with the whole class.
- Give out/display the Brian Patten poem and ask them to read it carefully.
- Ask them to answer the questions in Activity 5 individually. Call back their answers in a whole-class setting. Answers: (a) menial jobs as a cleaner; (b) he thought the questions were *simple* because they asked him to use his imagination; (c) personal answers; (d) because the Minister for Exams had a shallow soul, and didn't understand a child's imaginative answers.
- Ask students to get into their fours again and discuss Activity 6. Elicit their ideas. there are, of course, no right or wrong answers, however, one assumes that the Minister for Exams would have expected concrete, literal and definite answers rather than imaginative and allusive ones.

(continued on page 16)

1. What do you think about exams? Do you think they are a fair way of testing students' knowledge? Do you think there is a better way of doing that? How do you feel when you take an exam? Why do you think the education system uses exams? Think about your ideas, then discuss them in groups of four.

2. Look at the five questions below, think about them, then write a short answer to each of them on a separate piece of paper.
   Q1. Describe the taste of the moon.
   Q2. What colour is love?
   Q3. Why do snowflakes melt?
   Q4. Describe Adam's grief when he was expelled from Eden.
   Q5. What is the weight of an elephant's dream?

3. Get into a group of four and discuss your answers.

4. How do you feel about the questions? Which was the easiest and the most difficult to answer and why? Were they like the questions you usually get in school exams? If not, how were they different? What do exam questions usually test? What do you think these questions were testing? Think about your own answers to these questions, then discuss your ideas in your group of four.

5. Read Brian Patten's poem *The Minister for Exams* then answer the questions below.
   a) What does the narrator do now and why?
   b) What was his attitude to exams when he was a child? Why?
   c) What do you think about his answers to the questions?
   d) Why does he believe he failed the exams?

6. If the narrator's answers to Questions 1 to 3 were wrong, what do you think the correct answers were? Think about the answer to the question in the final line of the poem before you answer this.

7. Write three questions of your own like the ones the narrator answered as a child. Write each one on a separate piece of paper and give one to each member of your group to answer. Answer the three questions you are given.

So, for example, the answer to Question 1 could be : The taste of the moon is metallic rock and gritty, sandy dust.

- Ask the students to do the first part of Activity 7 individually, then get into their groups of four to give, receive and answer the questions.

Plenary (10 minutes)

- Have students read out questions and give answers around the class; you might like them to decide which were the best.
- Have a final discussion about what this poem tells us about exams and exam setters.

Homework

- Ask students to write a poem called 'The Minister for Homework'. You could give them the first lines, as follows, if you feel they need a start:

When I was a child I had to do homework.
Every night. Lots of it.
Homework 1: A page of arithmetic.
Homework 2: the life of Henry VII.
Homework 3:

Differentiation (of homework product): Students who don't like that title could invent their own 'Minister for . . .'

- It could be something connected to school (e.g. 'The Minister for School Dinners'; 'The Minster for PE'; 'The Minister for School Punishment')
- It could be something outside school (e.g. 'The Minister for Cycling'; 'The Minister for Rubbish . . .')

Classroom facts

Introduction: Students are to read and respond to the education of an earlier period by reading Charles Dickens's bitterly comic portrayal of a utilitarian classroom from *Hard Times*. The extract is slightly adapted from the original in that some short parts have been omitted in order to focus on the main interaction more clearly.

Aims and outcomes

- To read and appreciate a satirical piece of writing
- To analyse the language and ideas of an earlier period
- To compare students' own experience of education with that depicted

Resources required: The extract from Charles Dickens (1854) *Hard Times* (Resource Bank)

Lesson starter (10 minutes): Ask students to help you produce a time line of the history of education in Britain on the board. Start with private education for the rich, then Tudor grammar schools for the merchant classes, the rise of Sunday Schools, to the gradual introduction of schooling for all in Victorian times.

Main lesson (45 minutes)

- Hand out the task sheets. The students read the information in Activity 1, and respond to Activity 2 in pairs. (Answers: you might expect things like the range of different subjects, the general improvement of students' minds, the room for creative and original work.)
- In Activity 3 the students use only the knowledge they have in their heads.
- Give out the extract from *Hard Times* for them to read, and answer the question in Activity 4. (Answer: the insistence on *facts* with no room for *fancy* imagination.)
- Ask them to do Activity 5. You might read out Bitzer's definition, and then have some students read out their description. Ask for comments in relation to the questions.
- Activity 6. The students respond personally to the text. Open up a class discussion.
- Try to elicit the meanings of the 'difficult' words from context; it could also be used as a dictionary exercise. (Answers: (a) grass-eating; (b) fist-fighter (boxer); (c) fat; (d) approval; (e) weak ones who were last; (f) to imagine; (g) very pleased; (h) able to be)
- Activity 8. Students 'translate' longer passages of Victorian English to modern English. (Possible answers: *Why, then, you are not to see anywhere what you don't see in fact*: Well, then, you shouldn't see anything that you don't actually see; *Now I'll try you again*: Now, I'll test you again; *quite elated by coming so happily to his point*: very pleased to have got to his point so easily; *You are to be in all things regulated and governed by fact*: You must be controlled by fact in everything.)
- Activity 9. Students comment on the purpose of the text. (Answer: satire is making fun of something you find bad or ridiculous by exaggerating what it is like so that people laugh at it.)

Plenary (5 minutes): Students give examples of satire from TV, films, books, etc. (e.g. Orwell's *Animal Farm*; Malvolio in Shakespeare's *Twelfth Night*; the horror movie genre in Mel Brooks' *Young Frankenstein*, much of *Monty Python*; the business world in *The Office*).

Homework: Ask students to write a further classroom scene with Gradgrind and the government officer asking the class questions, in a similar style.

Differentiation: You may need to fill in some background on the Industrial Revolution and its effects if some students are not familiar with that period of British history.

1. Read the information below:
   Jeremy Bentham was a British thinker, whose ideas led to the spread of a theory of life called Utilitarianism. This was firmly rooted in the situation of the early nineteenth-century, with the industrialization of Britain, and the mass movement of people from the country to the town. This led to appalling conditions of work and living, for everyone, even young children. What little education there was aimed to fit children into being useful workers, consisted of teaching a basic ability to read, write and do simple maths, all of which would be necessary for working citizens. It was strictly factual, and 'utilitarian', that is, usefulness was the criterion by which everything was judged.

2. What things have you had in your own education that are different from the 'utilitarian' education described above? Discuss your ideas with a partner.

3. Imagine you are writing to someone who doesn't know what a horse is. Write a short description that would help them to understand all about the animal.

4. Read the extract from *Hard Times* by Charles Dickens, which describes a classroom scene. Decide what elements of 'utilitarian' education are shown in the extract. Discuss your ideas with a partner.

5. Compare your description of a horse to Bitzer's definition. In what ways are they the same or different? Would Mr Gradgrind have approved of what you wrote? Why/why not?

6. What are your feelings about Mr Gradgrind (who is the headteacher) and the government officer? What do you think about this type of education?

7. Look at the language Dickens uses. What do these words and phrases mean?
   a) gramnivorous
   b) pugilist
   c) corpulent
   d) approbation
   e) feeble stragglers
   f) to fancy
   g) elated
   h) susceptible

8. The language that we use now has changed from that which Dickens used in 1854. Find some phrases and sentences that we say differently, and 'translate' them into modern English.

   Example: *Girl number twenty possessed of no facts*
   Girl number twenty hasn't got any facts

9. 'In *Hard Times* Dickens satirizes the utilitarian ideals.' Explain this statement with reference to the passage you have just read.

In the playground

Introduction: This lesson uses a poem by Adrian Mitchell to explore the issue of bullying.

Aims and outcomes
- To read and understand a contemporary poem written in the form of a blues song
- To discuss its central topic of bullying

Resources required: You will need the poem 'Back in the Playground Blues' from Adrian Mitchell (1991) *Adrian Mitchell's Greatest Hits*. Newcastle-upon-Tyne: Bloodaxe Books. You can find it online at this address:

 http://uk.poetryinternationalweb.org/piw_cms/cms/cms_module/index.php?obj_id=13553

Additional musical activity (15 minutes): As an introduction, it might be a good idea to play the students a blues song which works in a similar form to the poem. *See* website for suggestions.

Lesson starter (15 minutes): Ask students about blues as a musical genre to establish some facts (e.g. USA; black musicians; from the start of nineteenth-century; typically slaves; bad working conditions such as cotton plantations; Mississippi; often songs of misery, but also up-tempo to feel happier; standard form: three-line verse with a repeated first line and rhyming third line; top UK performers now Eric Clapton, Gary Moore, Matt Scofield, Ian Siegal).

Main lesson (35 minutes)
- Activity 1. Students work in groups of 4. Elicit answers and try to establish general patterns (e.g. verbal bullying, continued threats, regular stealing or beating; the types of doers and victims; what students, teachers, 'the school' did about it) – examples can be from the local/national press, and your own school. List the responses for future reference.
- Give out/display the poem. Ask students to read it and then ask them how it links the two things you've been talking about (blues + bullying).
- Ask students to do Activity 3 individually, then discuss their answers in their group. Call back answers from the whole class. (Answers: (a) very large, fenced (so no escape), bad condition; (b) it sounds dangerous – not a place for 'playing'; (c) the safety of home is a long way away; (d) potentially, everyone; (e) because it can't be humiliated into begging for mercy; (f) an iceberg is cold, and ice makes a deep grinding sound as it crushes other ice, or destroys ships . . . icebergs are dangerous; (g) the idea is that the fight for survival strengthens one's inner reserves . . . though, of course, it terrifies and destroys the confidence of many.)
- The repeated second line in verses 1 and 2 emphasize, respectively, his small size, and the playgrounds large size. Also, the misery of the blues associated with the form is appropriate for the subject matter – the misery of being bullied.
- Activity 5 asks students, back in their groups of four, to come up with some concrete ways in which bullying can be stamped out.

Plenary (10 minutes): Elicit ideas from Activity 5 and make a whole class list. Discuss their practicalities, and what students can do on a daily basis.

Homework: Ask them to write a blues song about another aspect of their school life that they feel unhappy about (e.g. a subject they don't like, school dinners, homework . . .)

Differentiation: This lesson needs to be taken very seriously and treated carefully, as the class may contain both bullies and victims of bullying. Ensure students are fully aware of the awfulness of the situation.

TASK SHEET: **In the playground**

1. Think about some examples of bullying at school. What sort of people do the bullying? What sort of people are the victims? What is the reason for it? What are the outcomes? Get into a group of four and discuss your ideas.

2. Read the poem 'Back in the Playground Blues' by Adrian Mitchell.

3. Answer these questions about what is said:
    a) How is the playground described physically?
    b) What is the significance of the name it is called?
    c) Explain the intention of the first line of verse 3.
    d) Who *gets it* in this playground?
    e) Why is a beetle *not half the fun*?
    f) What do you understand by the first line of the last verse?
    g) The playground *prepares them for life*. How?
    Compare your answers in your group.

4. What is the effect of having the poem in the form of a blues song?

5. How can bullying be prevented? Discuss your ideas in groups of four. Come up with a list of five concrete proposals.

    1 _____

    2 _____

    3 _____

    4 _____

    5 _____

The school that I'd like

Introduction: In this lesson students will write a descriptive essay about their view of what school should be like. It follows on from the various school-related topics covered in the texts they have read in this section.

Aims and outcomes

* Students write a descriptive essay entitled 'The School That I'd Like'
* They do peer correction and write a second draft

Resources required: None.

Lesson starter (10 minutes): Ask students to think of one good and one bad thing about the school they attend. Open a class discussion. List their ideas in two columns on the board.

Main lesson (40 minutes)

* Hand out the task sheets and ask students to start completing the table in Activity 1, and then join in a group of four to brainstorm other ideas. Make sure that they realize that the basic nature of schooling has to stay the same, and the changes have to come inside that framework.
* Introduce them to the layout of the descriptive essay they are going to write. Ask them to make notes using the plan, based on the six areas they have already examined, discussed and noted. If there are other areas outside this, they should include them.
* Once they have planned their essay, they can write their first draft. Point out the example language in Activity 3, and go through it with students if you feel it necessary. Stress that they should start with the area they think most important in paragraph one and move towards the least important area in paragraph six. Decide if they are going to do the essay as classwork or homework.
* Once they have finished their first draft, they should work with a partner and do peer correction. Ask them to look at the organization of their partner's essay, and see that it hangs together and reads well. If they notice any language problems (e.g. spelling, incorrect tenses), they should underline them in pencil, and not correct them – the author should self-correct.
* When they have finished the peer correction, they should write a second draft, which will be given to you.

Plenary (10 minutes): Ask one or two students to read their work to the whole class. Encourage comments and discussion of the points that are made.

Differentiation: The whole lesson allows for differentiation of opinion about what is good/bad about school and offers individuals the opportunity to express their own ideas.

Homework: Based on the class discussion and their own ideas, ask students to prepare a list of changes that they believe are important and workable, and which could be presented to the school authorities for consideration as ways of improving the school. These can be discussed in a subsequent lesson, when a class 'master list' can be compiled and presented.

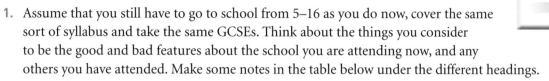

1. Assume that you still have to go to school from 5–16 as you do now, cover the same sort of syllabus and take the same GCSEs. Think about the things you consider to be the good and bad features about the school you are attending now, and any others you have attended. Make some notes in the table below under the different headings.

Teaching Rooms		Teachers		Hours/Time	
Good	Bad	Good	Bad	Good	Bad

Exams/Tests		Location of school		Facilities (e.g. Library/Gym)	
Good	Bad	Good	Bad	Good	Bad

Compare and share your ideas in a group of four.

2. Make notes for the first draft of your essay using the plan below. It is for the school magazine.

Title: The School That I'd Like

Opening statement:

Six paragraphs on the six areas in the table, with most important first.

1
2
3
4
5
6

Summary statement:

3. Language. Make sure you use appropriate discourse markers such as: *I think it would be better if . . . This would improve if . . . X could be improved by . . . I would prefer to . . . Most students would rather . . . X could be kept as it is . . . might stay the same, but . . . in my opinion... I like X, however it might be better to.. While A is a good idea, B should be . . .*

Section 2   The World of Work

To work or not to work?

Introduction: The poem 'Toads' was published in Philip Larkin's second collection *The Less Deceived* (London: Faber, 1955), and it explores his attitude to work. Larkin was a librarian all his life.

Aims and outcomes

- To introduce and discuss the topic of work
- To analyse the meaning and structure of a contemporary poem

Resources required: You will need the poem *Toads*, either from the original collection (*see* above) or from Anthony Thwaite (Ed.) (1988) *Philip Larkin: Collected Poems*. London: Faber. It is online at:

http://blue.carisenda.com/archives/cat_philip_larkin.html
http://plagiarist.com/poetry/4885/

You can hear the poem while the text scrolls on:

www.youtube.com/watch?v=T9xso6A_51w

Additional resources are suggested on the website.

Lesson starter (10 minutes): Ask students to decide individually what they think the best and worst jobs in the world are, and why. Call back ideas from the whole class and encourage discussion of the various suggestions.

Main lesson (40 minutes)

- Give out the task sheet and ask students to do Activity 1 individually and then discuss their ideas with a partner. Points you may want to draw out are the change from the 'survival work' (e.g. hunting, gathering) of our ancestors and some remaining ethnic groups in, say, the Amazon, and the 'paid work' of contemporary society. Also, you might build a board list of generic types of work (e.g. managerial, clerical, manual, skilled, unskilled, craft, education, medical, military, political, financial, agricultural, art, transport, computer, scientific, buying-selling . . .)
- Ask students to think about the quotations in Activity 2 individually, then discuss the questions with a partner. Background: Elbert Hubbard, USA, 1856–1915 (editor); Charles Baudelaire, France, (poet); Paul Tillich, German-USA, 1886–1965 (theologian/philosopher); Maxim Gorky, Russia, 1868–1936, (novelist). The Baudelaire quote is negative. The other three generally say that the right kind of work is a pleasure and central to human happiness and development.
- Distribute/display the poem 'Toads' and ask students to read it. Ask them to answer the question in Activity 4 immediately, without discussion. (Answer: he resents it.)
- Ask them to work through the questions in Activity 5 to explore the poem's meanings, individually or in pairs. (Answers: (a) because we generally dislike toads and think they are ugly; (b) *squat, brute, soils, sickening poison* build up a negative picture of 'the toad *work*' (c) *wit* – because wit implies brightness and intelligence, as opposed to the dullness of work; (d) to earn the money needed to survive; the amount of work done in order to gain enough money to survive; (e) *Lecturers* do intellectual work (not 'proper' work! – it's something of a joke to include them here); *lispers* are considered stupid because they can't speak correctly; *losels* are worthless people (archaic); *loblolly-men* are people acting as medical orderlies

(*continued on page 28*)

TASK SHEET: To work or not to work?

1. Think about work. Why do humans work? Broadly speaking, what different kinds of work are there? How is work different in different cultures? Is there such a thing as *good* work or b*ad* work? Discuss your ideas with a partner.

2. Read these quotations:

    'We work to become, not to acquire.'

    (Elbert Hubbard)

    'How many years of fatigue and punishment it takes to learn the simple truth that work, that disagreeable thing, is the only way of not suffering in life, or at all events, of suffering less.'

    (Charles Baudelaire)

    'The joy about our work is spoiled when we perform it not because of what we produce but because of the pleasure with which it can provide us, or the pain against which it can protect us.'

    (Paul Tillich)

    'When work is a pleasure, life is a joy. When work is a duty, life is slavery.'

    (Maxim Gorky)

    What do the four writers say about work? Which one shows a negative attitude? What is the general idea presented in the other three? Do you agree with what they say? Why/why not? Discuss your ideas with a partner.

3. Read the poem 'Toads' by Philip Larkin.

4. How would you sum up the poet's attitude to work?

5. Answer these questions about the subject of the poem:
   a) What is the significance of choosing a *toad* as a metaphor for work? List other words he uses to describe the *toad* in the first two verses. What effect do they have?
   c) What does he set in opposition to *the toad work*? Why?
   d) What does he see as the purpose of work? What is *out of proportion*?
   e) In verse 3 he lists people he considers don't work. What are they? How do they survive?
   f) What sort of people is he describing in verses 4 and 5?
   g) What would he like to do in verse 6, and why won't he? Do you recognize, or can you find the source of, the quotation used in the final two lines of this verse?
   h) What does he say about himself and his attitude to work in verses 7 and 8?
   i) What do you understand from the final verse?

6. Answer these questions about the structure of the poem and techniques used in it:
   a) What is the verse form?
   b) Does it rhyme? If not, what does it do? Give some examples. Look at verse 3. What technique is used? What is its effect? Where else in the poem is this technique used?

7. Summarize the poet's attitude to work in 50 words:

   _____
   _____
   _____
   _____
   _____
   _____

8. Relate the poet's view of work to those expressed in the four quotations in Activity 2.

on ships – not properly qualified; *louts* are crude, oafish people – so generally people with no standing; (f) poor homeless people, living outside society; (g) to give up his job and do nothing – because he knows it isn't realistic; the quotation comes from *The Tempest* Act IV, Scene 1, and is spoken by Prospero; (h) he has a work-ethic inside him that won't allow him to use his wit (*blarney*) to escape; (i) that maybe wit and work aren't really part of the same thing, but if you have both inside you, you can't lose just one of them.)

- Ask students to do Activity 5, individually, or in pairs. (Answers: (a) nine four-line verses; (b) it doesn't rhyme (except for *enough/stuff* in verse 6), but has and A-C/B-D 'chime' scheme – what is commonly known as pararhyme (e.g. *bucket/like it; wives/starves*); (c) alliteration; the /l/ sound (in *Lots-live-Lecturers-lispers-losels-loblolly-men-louts*) – particularly because *loblolly* has the sound three times – make it sound foolish. Alliteration is also used in the third line of verse 7, with the dull thud of the /h/ sound making the toad seem solid and fixed.

- Students write a 50-word summary. They can then exchange their work for a peer correction of language and ideas. Fifty words should be four or five sentences. They need to include the following ideas: the poet resents work, and wishes he didn't have to do it; he feels he has to work too much to get the money he needs to survive; he wishes he could escape, because plenty of others survive without doing work; he realizes that he won't give up work, because he has the work ethic inside him.

Plenary (10 minutes): Activity 8 will serve as a good way to round off the lesson with the whole class, pointing out Larkin's negative attitude chiming with Baudelaire's, and finding none of the pleasure the other three extol.

Homework: Students are to write about their future hopes for work – what they would like to do, and why it would make them happy.

Differentiation: Account needs to be taken of the students' different home experience of work, depending on their parents' situations: you might have anyone in class from the child of a managing director to the child of the long-term unemployed. Let them all have their say about work at the appropriate time.

Introduction: This lesson uses the Simon Armitage poem 'Night Shift' (from *Zoom!* (1989) Newcastle-upon-Tyne: Bloodaxe Books) to examine the effect of work on people and their relationships.

Aims and outcomes
- To discuss attitudes to work
- To examine a poem and relate it personal ideas

Resources required: The poem can be found in the original collection it came from (*see* above), and also in Hulse M/Kennedy D/Morley D (Eds) (1993) *The New Poetry*. Newcastle-upon-Tyne: Bloodaxe Books. The author can be heard reading it on CD1 of the *Poetry Please Anniversary Anthology*.

Lesson starter (10 minutes): Bring in a recent newspaper headline related to work in the UK (e.g. a factory closure), and/or play a related TV or radio clip. Ask students what they know about it and how the people affected feel.

Main lesson (40 minutes)
- Give out the handout; ask students to consider the questions in Activity 1 individually, then discuss their ideas in a group of four. Call back ideas from the whole class, and compile a word bank on the board of feelings and emotions (e.g. exhausted, depressed, resigned, frustrated, angry, anxious). Expand their vocabulary away from the obvious, so if a student says 'tired' ask for synonyms (e.g. exhausted, weary), and add these to the word bank beside the initial word.
- Ask them to think about the questions in Activity 2 individually, then discuss their ideas in their group of four. They should pool their insights into the table on the task sheet, and each student should have a copy.
- Number the students in each group one to four, and then have all the ones together, the twos and so on, to exchange their groups ideas and note those of other groups.
- Display or hand out the 'Night Shift' poem and ask students to read it, then do Activity 4 on their task sheet immediately. (Answer: The narrator comes home from *working on the night shift* and finds that his wife *has already left* the house. He knows this because in the kitchen he can see *the steam on the kettle* and hear *water still moving in the pipes*. In the living room he notices *that dust has been moved when she opened the curtains* and can hear *the metal in the cooling paraffin heater contracting*. In the bedroom he can smell his wife's *hairspray in the air* and when he gets into bed he finds that *her body warmth is still inside the duvet*.)
- Ask students to reread the poem and answer the questions in Activity 5. They can confer with a partner when they've decided individually. (Answers: The narrator works on the night shift somewhere, and his wife works a normal day shift, so they never meet each other. They have written messages to each other in lipstick on the bathroom mirror. That they are working hard to pay for a house for them to be in together, but that same work keeps them apart.)
- Activity 6 asks students to make a connection between their thoughts on the effects of work and this situation. They can discuss it with a partner before you ask the class for suggestions.
- The next three activities work on the text as a poem. Activity 7 answer: it is written in strict 10-syllable lines. Activity 8 answer: *kettle-level-unsettled; clockwork-woken; woken-written; paid for-mirror-other; hairspray-duvet* even manages a rhyme.
- In Activity 9 ask students to give you some words and feelings about the poem. You might get responses such as: *simple – limited – muted – resigned – sad – downbeat*. Ask how this

(continued on page 32)

TASK SHEET: **The effects of work**

1. Think about what effects work has on people. Think about how they feel at the end of the day, the end of the week, at the start of their annual holidays. Think about more serious effects when companies go bankrupt and workers are laid off in a recession. Make some notes, then discuss your ideas in a group of four.

2. What do people work for? Imagine yourself in ten years time, with a partner; you both have jobs. How will you use the money you earn? Think about short-term and long-term plans. Discuss these things in a group of four, and make a list in the table below.

Short-term use of earnings	Long-term use of earnings

3. Read the poem 'Night Shift' by Simon Armitage.

4. Complete the following passage about the facts of the situation.

> The narrator comes home from _____ and finds that his wife _____ the house. He knows this because in the kitchen he can see _____ and hear _____. In the living room he notices _____ and can hear _____. In the bedroom he can smell his wife's _____ and when he gets into bed he finds that _____.

5. What is the working situation of the narrator and his wife? How have they communicated? What is the irony about their situation?

6. Relate the content of the poem to what you discussed in Activity 1 and 2.

7. Apart from being written in couplets, there is a major underlying structure to this poem. Can you find out what it is?

8. 'There is a vague sense of unforced pararhyme in this poem.' Illustrate this statement.

9. How would you describe the tone of this poem?

10. Role-play. Work in a pair. One of you is the narrator, the other his wife. You finally meet over Sunday breakfast, when he gets home from work and she doesn't have to go to work. You are both fed-up with the situation. Work out a dialogue discussion of the situation and how you might resolve it. perform your role-play for another pair.

is achieved (through reference to objects rather than people, and by no anger shown at the situation or loud happiness at the positives of the last two verses). It is all very factual and neutral.

- In Activity 10, you should pair the students (boy-girl if possible) to role-play the situation described. You might brainstorm some of the things they would be likely to discuss (their anger, frustration; the need to change jobs; pay; mortgage payments; finances in general). Have the pairs practise a few times – they can write a note-form dialogue if they wish – then they can 'perform' it for another pair.

Plenary (10 minutes): Discuss the couple's situation with the whole class. What could they do to improve it?

Homework: Ask students to write a 200-word analysis and commentary on the poem, using the ideas raised in the lesson.

Differentiation: The role-play activity allows for different responses to the situation to be expressed and to meet, clash negotiate and compromise.

Town and country

Introduction: This lesson centres on 'The Dalesman's Litany' by Frederck William Moorman (1872–1919). He wrote it as a Yorkshire dialect poem, although most modern renderings of it have been considerably cleaned up. It deals with the idea of moving for work, which is, of course, a big contemporary issue.

Aims and outcomes

- To examine an older text (plus song), which is also regional
- To link earlier British migrations from country to tow in the Industrial Revolution to contemporary migrations into the UK (e.g. the Poles in the early noughties)

Resources required: The original version of the poem in full Yorkshire dialect alongside a 'cleaned-up' version can be found on:

 www.informatik.uni-hamburg.de/~zierke/steeley.span/songs/thedalesmanslitany.html

It is recommended that you use the 'cleaned-up' version, unless you're actually teaching in Yorkshire, or deliberately want to expose your students to a strong dialect. There are a number of sung versions of it, using the music written by Dave Keddie in the 1960s. These can be watched by typing 'The Dalesman's Litany' into YouTube. For additional musical suggestions *see* the website.

Lesson starter (10 minutes): Ask students if they have ever met anyone who came to Britain to work; failing this, ask whether they know of current situations where economic migration has taken place. Open a class discussion on the situations such people find themselves in. If some related event has been in the news locally or nationally, then bring in newspaper articles or recordings of TV or radio news.

Main lesson (40 minutes)

- Hand out the task sheet and ask students to think about the questions in Activity 1 and discuss them with a partner. Call back answers from the whole class. Answers: generally, people from the country moved into the larger industrial towns to work in factories.
- Ask the pairs to consider the points in Activity 2, make notes and then share them in a whole class setting. The workplaces were dangerous, noisy; the pay was poor – no pay if you were ill; work damaged health; very long hours; living conditions dreadful – cramped, unsanitary.
- Hand out/show the poem. Ask students what the title means. A *dalesman* is someone from the agricultural Yorkshire Dales; a litany is an invocation, usually religious – asking for God's help. Ask them to read the poem.
- Once read, ask students to do Activity 4 individually, then compare their answers with a partner. (Answers: (a) Yorkshire – the names of the places, *ridings*; (b) because the landowner he works for won't give him married accommodation; (c) went to sea, worked in a mill, worked as a blacksmith (forge), worked in a steel plant (furnace), worked in a coal mine (pits); (d) Sheffield = *Hell*; the fire and noise of the furnaces; the pits were full of *muck*; leeds was foggy; people lived in cramped conditions (coop); snow *black as ebony* with soot; (e) his children grew up and left home and he and his wife returned to the Dales, away from the industry.)
- Activity 5 could be done as homework, or using GoogleMaps on an interactive whiteboard.
- Ask students to consider this and discuss ideas with a partner. List ideas from the whole class on the board. (Answer: he is resourceful, hard-working, honest, brave, caring [of his family].)
- Ask students to do Activity 7 as a dictionary exercise if they are not familiar with the words.

(continued on page 36)

TASK SHEET: **Town and country**

1. What do you know about the Industrial Revolution, and movements of people in Britain from the late eighteenth-century until the late nineteenth-century? Who went where, and why? Discuss your ideas with a partner.

2. What were conditions like for people who worked in Victorian factories? Think about the workplace itself, pay, hours, health and living conditions. Make notes under these headings and then share them with a partner.

3. Read the words of a poem called 'The Dalesman's Litany' written by Frederick William Moorman (1872–1919), which talks about the situation in which country people often found themselves in the nineteenth-century. Make sure you know what a *dalesman* and a *litany* are before you start to read it.

4. Answer these questions:
   a) Which part of England does it take place in? Give reasons for your answer.
   b) Why does the protagonist have to go to work in the town?
   c) What different jobs did he do? Make a list of them.
   d) Find some phrases that indicate the conditions in which he lived and worked.
   e) What happens in the end?

5. Find a map and locate all the places which are mentioned in the poem.

6. Given what he did and the end of the story, what words would you use to describe the protagonist?

7. What is the meaning of these words and phrases?
   a) verse 1, line 4: *I'd bide*
   b) verse 2, line 2: *squire*
   c) verse 3, line 2: *I've addled honest brass*
   d) verse 4, line 4: *fell*
   e) verse 5, line 1: *brig*
   f) verse 5, line 5: *beck*
   g) verse 6, line 4: *slack*
   What relation do some of them have to your answer to question 4a? Discuss your answers with a partner.

8. What makes the refrain *From Hull and Halifax and Hell/Good Lord deliver me* such an effective piece of language?

9. What is the structure of the verses?

10. What situations can you think of in contemporary society – British and elsewhere – where people move in order to work?

(Answers: (a) live; (b) landowner; (c) earned honest money; (d) hills; (e) bridge; (f) river; (g) coal spoil heaps (NB in the 'modern' version it says *stack*). They are Yorkshire words.)

- Ask students to think about this individually, then discuss it with a partner. (Answer: it alliterates, and *Hull* and *Hell* are almost the same word; also there is the surprise of having *Hell* after the names of two Yorkshire towns.)
- Activity 9. (Answer: ABCBDEFE)
- Activity 10. Try to relate this economic migration to what has happened recently in the UK and elsewhere. Novels such as Rose Tremain's *The Road Home* and Marina Lewycka's *Two Caravans* have dealt with Poles in this situation.

Plenary (10 minutes): Play one of the sung versions of the song, while they follow the words. Ask them to consider whether it works better as a song or a poem. Possible answers: the refrain at the end of each verse makes it more like a song. Also it sounds like a traditional industrial folk song.

Homework: Ask students to imagine that the protagonist was working somewhere away from his wife, Mary Jane – they can choose where, and what job he was doing. They should write a letter from him to her, detailing what he is doing, the conditions, and so on.

Diversity: You may have students in your class whose families are economic migrants, and so you may be able to find out about first-hand experiences from them.

Other people's jobs

Introduction: In this lesson, students will examine a specific job (that of a security guard), which they may not have thought much about, through a weekend newspaper magazine article.

Main aims and outcomes
- To think and talk about the work of a little-discussed job
- To work on and appreciate a piece of journalistic prose

Resources required: The article on 'Security guards' by Craig Taylor from *The Guardian Weekend* magazine (13.06.09), which is available on *The Guardian* website at the following address:

 www.guardian.co.uk/lifeandstyle/2009/jun/13/take-10-security-guards

Lesson starter (10 minutes): Tell students that we often talk and write about jobs like being a doctor, teacher, manager, actor, footballer . . . but many jobs are never mentioned. Ask for examples of such jobs and list them on the board.

Main lesson (40 minutes)
- Hand out the task sheet. Students do Activity 1 individually and Activity 2 in fours. Elicit ideas from the whole class and open a discussion; you might ask them to decide what the 'best' and 'worst' jobs are.
- In Activity 3 they focus on particular aspects of the job individually, then in fours. Note answers from the class on the board.
- Hand out the *Security Guards* article and ask the students to read it. Work with the whole class to compare their ideas from Activity 3 to what they have read. You can circle the things they mentioned on the board, and add other points raised in the article which they missed.
- Activity 5. Students read and answer questions about the content. (Answers: (a) that you need to understand people's behaviour to be a good security guard; (b) to let people enjoy themselves without danger; (c) negatively, as violent, criminal or obsessive body-builders; (d) the Private Security Industry Act of 2001; the number of unregistered immigrants working as security guards; (e) it's more discreet, smarter, with no overt violence; (f) that security guards have to understand situations and sense when something is different about people's behaviour; (g) because it is fast, and efficient and can sniff out things that a human can't.)
- Activity 6. Vocabulary work, possibly with a dictionary. (Answers: (a) angry person who had been thrown out of a club; (b) obsessive body-builders who use steroids to enhance their muscles; (c) security for large companies; (d) secret trips; (e) won't be affected by a general fall in prices; (f) to take place, happen; (g) illegal products, such as drugs or explosives.)
- Activity 7 looks at genre, purpose, style. (Answers: it's from a newspaper weekend magazine; middle-class public; it gives limited background information; the style is easy journalese – some quotations give a 'researched' feel; real names make it seem authentic; not a detailed study.)

Plenary (10 minutes): Activity 8. Students pull all their ideas and the class discussions together to give a personal take on the pros and cons of being a security guard.

Homework: Students write 200 words on 'Last Night at the Flamingo Club', which should be an account of a night's work as a security guard at a club door.

Differentiation: Allow students who know security guards and have experience of them at work to contribute their valuable first-hand experience to discussions.

TASK SHEET: Other people's jobs

1. Think about all the different jobs there are in the world. In the table below list three full-time jobs you would really like to do and three you would really hate to do. Have reasons why for each one.

Three jobs I'd really like to do	Three jobs I'd really hate to do
1.	1.
2.	2.
3.	3.

2. Work in a group of four, and ask and answer questions about your choices. Try to agree on a group *best* and *worst* job.

3. Think about the job of a security guard. What different types of security guards are there? What does their work involve? Who do they work for? When do they work? What do they look like? How do you view this job? Make some notes, then compare your ideas in a group of four.

4. Read the article about security guards. How did the things the writer says compare with your ideas about the job?

5. Read the article again and answer these questions:
   a) What does the opening speech imply about the job?
   b) What is the object of a club doorman's job?
   c) In general, how do the public perceive security guards?
   d) In the last ten years, what has improved the profession, and what has weakened it?
   e) How is bodyguarding different from lower levels of security work?
   f) What do you understand by *aware of the absence of the normal*?
   g) Why is a guard dog useful?

6. What do these words and phrases mean?
   a) *irate ejectee*
   b) *steroid-addled gym-nuts*
   c) *corporate protection*
   d) *clandestine visits*
   e) *recession-proof*
   f) *pan out*
   g) *banned substances*

   Check your answers with a partner.

7. Where do you think this article came from and who do you think it was written for? What is it's purpose? How would you describe the style of the writing?

8. Do you think you would like to work as a security guard? If so, at which level, and why? If not, why not? Tell the members of your group.

Working children

Introduction: This is another lesson that relates to an earlier period, and can be linked to 2.3 'The Dalesman's Litany' and 1.6 *Hard Times*, through the topic of the conditions of life in the eighteenth and nineteenth-centuries. This one looks at the issue of child labour through William Blake's poem 'The Chimney Sweeper'.

Aims and outcomes
* To analyse a classic poem, its form, language and ideas
* To discuss the topic of child labour

Resources required: You can find the poem in William Blake (1966) *Complete Writings*. Oxford: Oxford University Press, or online at:

 http://rpo.library.utoronto.ca/poem/165.html
www.enotes.com/chimney-sweeper-text

The poem is read on YouTube with a still picture at

 www.youtube.com/watch?v=ssjjOqr_cLg&NR=1

and performed live at:

 www.youtube.com/watch?v=JC4D2scQDI&feature=related

Lesson starter (15 minutes): Ask students what they know about the labour laws regarding children working in the UK. Ask if they think this is the same everywhere in the world, and invite examples. Ask if this was the same in the UK historically, and invite information about the situation in Victorian and earlier times (UK laws can be found on the website.)

Main lesson (35 minutes)
* Hand out the task sheet and ask students to consider and discuss the questions in Activity 1 – you can do this as a whole-class activity. (Answers: when the UK was heated exclusively by coal and wood fires, the chimney sweep was essential – blocked chimneys caused fires; in earlier times, young children had to climb inside networks of chimneys in city tenements and large houses – only they would fit inside; children often died young through inhaling soot, ill-health, poor living conditions etc.; extending brushes could be used for smaller chimneys; modern equipment makes the process cleaner, using vacuum pumps.)
* Give out/display the poem for students to read. They can then answer the questions in Activity 3 individually, and compare their answers with a partner. (Answers: (a) a boy chimney sweeper; (b) his father sold him to a Master Sweep after his mother died; (c) He comforts him because he's a new smaller boy; (d) Tom Dacre; (e) they run to the river and wash themselves, to clean off the soot; (f) because the Angel told him God was his father, so he could be happy; (g) that people should do as they told, not complain, be 'good' and everything will be alright – you'll go to heaven)
* The irony is that the young narrator couldn't even talk properly when he was sold, and instead of calling out 'Sweep, sweep!' in the streets he called 'Weep, weep!', and of course, he probably wept a lot at his miserable existence, and it made others weep to see the child sweeps.
* (Answer: It is a six-verse poem, with four lines per verse. They are mostly in correct AABB rhyme scheme; in verse 5 the noun *wind* was pronounced like the verb 'to wind a watch' in Blake's time and so would have rhymed with *behind*; in verse 6, while *warm* may have been

(continued on page 42)

TASK SHEET: **Working children**

1. What do you know about the work of a chimney sweep? What do they have to do, and how do they do it? What equipment do they use? In what ways do you think a modern chimney sweep's work is different to one in the eighteenth and nineteenth-centuries?

2. Read the poem 'The Chimney Sweeper' by William Blake.

3. Answer these questions:
   a) Who is the narrator of the poem?
   b) How did he become a chimney sweep?
   c) What does the narrator do to Tom in verse 2?
   d) Who had a dream?
   e) What do the sweeps do immediately after they are set free? Why?
   f) Why does Tom feel better the morning after the dream?
   g) What does the last line mean?
   Discuss your answers with a partner.

4. In the eighteenth and nineteenth-centuries, it was common for people to walk around the streets calling out the services or things they had to sell (rather like an ice-cream van these days plays a tune to let people know it's there). So a fruit seller might call out 'Fresh apples! Fresh apples for sale!", and a knife-sharpener 'Knives! Bring out your knives!' What do you think a chimney sweep might have called out? Now think about what the narrator says in lines 2 and 3 of the first verse, and see how Blake uses it ironically. Compare your ideas with a partner.

5. What is the structure of the poem?

6. How do the symbols of black-white run through the poem, and what do they mean?

7. Why do you think Blake published a poem like this in 1789?

8. The poem was published in a collection called *Songs of Innocence*. What is 'innocent' about this poem?

pronounced to rhyme with *harm* in Blake's time, *dark* and *work* don't rhyme – they chime (pararhyme); it has a variable syllable structure, but with 10, 11 (mostly) and 12 syllables, and just verse 1 line 3 with 8 syllables.)

- The black-white symbols are fairly obvious. (Answers: *soot* is black; everything black is negative – *I sleep in soot; the soot cannot spoil your white hair* – beautiful hair is compared to a lamb's (innocence), which black spoils; the sweeps in the dream are in *coffins of black*; the Angel has a *bright* key (bright = white); when the sweeps have washed, they *shine in the sun* and are *naked and white* (bright = white = pure = positive) – the unstated obvious is that they have washed off the black soot; they *rose in the dark* (negative = still night = work = black).)
- (Possible answer: because he was horrified at what industrialization was doing to Britain and wanted people to take note of the plight of the people.)
- The naivety of the child who thinks 'everything will be all right' because he is looked after by God and will have a happy time after death, when in fact his current life is absolutely miserable.

Plenary (10 minutes): Ask students to discuss whether they think poems, or literature in general, can ever bring about change in society.

Homework: Imagine you are a social reformer in Victorian Britain. Write a letter to a newspaper about the conditions of child chimney sweeps.

Differentiation (of homework): If students would prefer to write a letter to a newspaper about some other – perhaps contemporary – aspect of child labour, let them do so. In either case, they will be able to research some facts on the internet.

Manufacturing biscuits

Introduction: The students are going to look at the process of developing a new type of biscuit, and then develop one of their own on the same basis.

Aims and outcomes
- To read and understand an essay on modern manufacturing processes
- To work in a group to develop their own product
- To make a presentation of their product to the whole class

Resources required (15 minutes): The text extract from Chapter 3 'Biscuit Manufacture' from Alain de Botton (2009) *The Pleasures and Sorrows of Work*. London: Hamish Hamilton, a series of essays on different kinds of work (Resource Bank).

Lesson starter: Ask students to think and then say what their favourite type of sweet biscuit is, and why they like that best. Elicit answers from around the class. If possible, bring in enough packets of McVitie's Moments into class (at nine biscuits per box, three will provide for a class of 27 . . . they could have half of one each!); ask students if they know these biscuits, if they've tried them; if there are students who have, get them to tell the class what they're like. Then let all students try them and tell you what they think about them. Tell them that they were developed to appeal to one sector of the public in particular, and invite them to suggest which one, and why. (Don't give the answer – they'll get it in the text.)

Main lesson (Activities 1–7: 40 minutes; Activity 8: 40 minutes, plus presentation time)
- Hand out the task sheet, and ask students to do Activity 1 in pairs. Call back answers from the whole class, and list them on the board; try to organize the board – eliciting headings from the students – into different areas of work (e.g. management, production, logistics, design) with the various relevant jobs underneath them.
- Hand out/display the text 'Manufacturing biscuits'. Ask students to read it and answer Activity 3. (Answers: jobs listed in the text are: branding expert, designer, executive, manger of forklift truck fleet, packaging technologist, branding executive, learning centre manager, strategic projects evaluator.). Call back answers and compare them with the list on the board. Produce a definitive list, after due discussion.
- This activity asks for close reading for information. Call back answers from the whole class. (Answers: the gathering of 'low-income' women at the hotel. The discovery of their dissatisfactions, the production of moments on the basis of this.)
- Students examine a specific simile (Answers: It is can have the same effects as such a protagonist – this is related to the kind of name we typically find in novels by Dickens and other Victorian novelists, where the name (e.g. *Gradgrind*) reflects the person's character. The biscuit is thus a 'characterful' product).
- Activity 6 looks specifically at a number of important language elements in the text. (Answers: (a) in trying to pull put out of them some of their personal desires; (b) aphorism (a short, pithy and amusing statement; *brevity* = shortness.); (c) complete decadence was not being asked for; (d) a style of handwriting from an earlier period; (e) the whole reason for everyone working as they should is the production of biscuits; (f) the science of checking that biscuits with wafer biscuits in them don't destroy each other while being transported.
- This is an important stage in working towards their final goal. The stages are as follows: 1 – gather interviewees and question them; 2 – decide on the shape of the biscuit;

(*continued on page 46*)

TASK SHEET: **Manufacturing biscuits**

1. 'United Biscuits' is a large company that produces sweet biscuits and savoury snacks. It employs 5,000 people. Work with a partner to produce a list of all the different jobs which you think such a company needs.

2. Read the text 'Manufacturing biscuits' by Alain de Botton.

3. How many of the jobs you listed are mentioned? Add any others you missed to your list. Do you think this is a complete list now?

4. Laurence tells the author that 'Biscuits nowadays are a branch of psychology'. How does the text go on to show that this is true?

5. What is meant by the new biscuit being 'as subtly and appropriately nuanced as that of a protagonist in a great novel'?

6. Look at these words and phrases and decide what they mean:
   a) *in an attempt to tease out of them certain emotional longings*
   b) *with aphoristic brevity*
   c) *it was not outright decadence that was being evoked*
   d) *a romantic Edwardian script*
   e) *all employment at the company was ultimately predicated on the sale of confectionery*
   f) *how to ensure a minimum of friction between wafers during transit*
   Discuss your answers with a partner.

7. Make a flow chart showing the sequence of six stages which went on in the two years that Laurence was developing *Moments*.

8. Imagine that you had to work for United Biscuits, and that you were able to do any job you wanted within the company. What would you choose and why? Tell a partner.

9. Work in a group of four. You are a biscuit company. Choose a name. You are going to develop a new biscuit which will appeal to the 14–16 age group. Go through the stages you listed in Activity 6, and come up with a product. You are then going to make a presentation to the rest of the class; each of your group must speak in the presentation, and you should illustrate it appropriately.

3 – decide on the contents of the biscuit; 4 – packaging; 5 – name the biscuits; 6 – decide on fonts for the print on the packages.)

- Activity 8 allows students to decide how they might relate to a company like United Biscuits. It is a personal choice, but fundamentally there is room for everyone to work under such an umbrella.
- The final activity is the preparation for a huge role-play, which needs handling carefully by you. Ask students to work closely to achieve a suitable presentation; offer them the technology they need for their presentations, if possible: computers, beamers, OHPs/pens; flipcharts; large paper and colours, etc.).

Plenary (30 minutes/variable – depending on number of groups): Students present their product. Other groups decide which is the best product/best presentation.

Homework: Students write 150–200 words about working in the mining industry.

Differentiation: Students get a chance to interact in ways which are very different from their normal discourse. In this way, they will play 'beyond and outside' themselves.

A country craft

Introduction: A look at thatching through the eyes of Nobel laureate, Seamus Heaney.

Main aims and objectives
- To explore a classic piece of contemporary poetry
- To describe, in prose, a manual process

Resources required: The poem 'Thatcher' from Seamus Heaney (1969) *Door into the Dark*. London: Faber. Find it online at:

 http://listsearches.rootsweb.com/th/read/IrelandGenWeb/2002–12/1039459721

Lesson starter (10 minutes): Ask students to list some country crafts and associated jobs (e.g. thatching/thatcher; barrel-making/cooper), and say what is happening to them and why (e.g. they're disappearing because they're no longer necessary; problems finding apprentices).

Main lesson (40 minutes)
- Hand out the task sheet. Ask students to pool their knowledge of thatching. List what you call back from the whole class on the board. Leave the list there until they have done Activity 3.
- Give out/display the poem 'Thatcher' by Seamus Heaney and ask students to read it.
- Activity 3. Students list material and equipment and compare with their ideas in Activity 1. (Answers: equipment: *light ladder, bag of knives, well-honed blades;* and he makes *a white-pronged staple*; materials: *sheaves of lashed wheat-straw, bundled rods: hazel and willow.*)
- Activity 4 could be a dictionary activity if you wish. (Answers: (a) booked, ordered; (b) the part of the roof that projects beyond the wall; (c) well-sharpened; (d) lying down (term from heraldry); (e) cut so they were the same length; (f) the ends; (g) to make something golden – from the myth; (h) a twig bent to a U-shape, with sharpened (thus white) ends; (i) the remains of straw stalks when they are cut.)
- This activity asks students to identify process discourse markers (first-then-next-after that-finally) used in Heaney's description of thatching. (Answer: *Next, the bundled rods; Then fixed the ladder.*)
- Activity 6 asks students to analyse the style of writing Heaney uses, particularly in lines 4–14. (Answers: *eyed-poked-opened-handled-flicked-twisted-fixed-laid out-snipped-sharpened-shaved -flushed-stitched.* The verbs show the thatching process, the constant action.)
- Activity 7 asks for the explanation of figures of speech. (Answers: the roof is described as being *a sloped honeycomb* and *a stubble patch*, because of the texture that is visible; the thatcher's *Midas touch* is that he made the roof golden with the new thatch. *Them* are the people who have been watching the work, and they are *gaping* in admiration at the beautiful, neat result.)
- In this activity students examine a couple key phrases. (Answers: (a) the thatcher's *world* is the roof above the ground, and he – and the thatch – needs to be pinned for security reasons; (b) lying down on the roof is necessary to do the work – it's unusual to use *couchant* which is a term from heraldry, usually referring to lions.)
- In Activity 9 students analyse the poem's form. (Answers: the poem has 4-line verses in a rather loose AABB chime-scheme (e.g. *wheat-straw/willow*); 10 syllables for lines 1-11, 16; 11 syllables for lines 12-15; iambic pentameter; in-verse and across-verse enjambment.)

Plenary (10 minutes): 'The poem is an allegory about writing a poem.' Ask students to discuss how it might work (e.g. taking different materials and crafting them into something, using a *Midas touch* that leaves people *gaping*; poetry is a craft, too.)

Homework: Activity 10. Emphasize the need to use process discourse markers.

Differentiation: Students can choose any manual process they know well for their writing.

TASK SHEET: **A country craft**

1. Think about the craft of thatching a roof. How is it done? What materials and equipment are needed? Discuss your ideas with a partner.

2. Read the poem 'Thatcher' by Irish poet Seamus Heaney.

3. List the equipment and materials that the thatcher brings with him. Check it against your own list from Activity 1.

4. Check that you understand these words and phrases:
   a) *Bespoke*
   b) *eaves*
   c) *well-honed*
   d) *Couchant*
   e) *flushed*
   f) *butts*
   g) *Midas touch*
   h) *a white-pronged staple*
   i) stubble
   Compare with your partner.

5. In this poem Heaney describes the process the thatcher goes through; when we describe a process, we use a set of well-known discourse markers (e.g. First . . . after that . . . finally). Heaney doesn't actually use these examples, but he uses two others to indicate the stages. What are they?

6. 'The poem is all about verbs of action.' Explain and illustrate this statement.

7. Explain the three metaphors used in the last sentence of the poem. Who are the *them*, and why were they *gaping*?

8. What is the significance of these phrases?
   a) *for pinning down his world*
   b) *couchant for days*

9. Describe the formal structure of the poem.

10. Think of a manual process that you know well – for example, doing the washing in a machine at home – and describe it in detail, mentioning all the things you need, and using suitable discourse markers to structure your writing.

That isn't a real job!

Introduction: This lesson uses an amusing poem about a businessman's attitude to poets.

Aims and outcomes
- To read and enjoy a 'light' poem, which is also, however, an attack on attitudes to poetry
- To write a monologue attacking an imaginary person in a job they think is worthless

Resources required: The poem 'What the Chairman Told Tom' from Richard Caddel (Ed.) (2000) *Basil Bunting: Complete Poems.* Tarset: Bloodaxe Books, also anthologized in: Shapcot J/Sweeney M (Eds) (1996) *Emergency Kit: poems for Strange Times.* London: Faber. It was first published in 1965. You can find it online at:

www.poetryfoundation.org/archive/poem.html?id=177188
www.poemhunter.com/poem/what-the-chairman-told-Tom

Lesson starter (20 minutes)
- Put the students into three groups of ten (if you have fewer than 30, give out fewer jobs, starting with Librarian and Shopkeeper, but never take out poet). Give each student a slip of paper with one of the jobs on it: DOCTOR/LAWYER/TEACHER/BANKER/SOLDIER/ FOOTBALLER/ FARMER/LIBRARIAN/SHOPKEEPER/POET. Tell them they are the last ten people alive in a bomb shelter, but they only have enough food for five to survive until it is safe to go outside again. In turn they argue why it is vital for them to stay in the shelter. Then they vote on which five have to leave. Afterwards, discuss what the groups decided and why.

Main lesson (35 minutes)
- Activity 1. Students discuss their feelings about writers in general and poets in particular, their work and value to society.
- Students read the Basil Bunting poem 'What the Chairman Told Tom'.
- Activity 3. Students complete the table with facts and their own ideas, then check with a partner. (Answers: The Chairman: accountant, £3000 pa, car, vouchers, owns the company, ten-year-old daughter, runs model trains, doesn't like words – only understands material things, doesn't appreciate art and creativity; Mr Shaw: an employee, keeps pigeons – obedient employee; Nancy: was in the chorus of 'The Desert Song' – secretary? Chairman's wife; Mr Hines: a teacher, doesn't like 'modern' poetry – perhaps the Chairman's daughter's teacher?; Tom: poet, has suggested he works for the company at £12 per week, poetry doesn't rhyme, he's married – he's proactive, trying to make a living out of poetry.)
- Activity 4. The global scenario. (Answer: Tom has just asked the Chairman to employ him as company poet at £12 a week; the Chairman explains why he won't employ Tom.)
- Activity 5. Specific meanings. (Answers: He implies that (a) poetry isn't Art; (b) a bus conductor doesn't earn much for a more important job; (c) accountants get a high salary because they do a worthwhile job; (d) his poetry is no good because it doesn't rhyme; (e) he feels dirty being near a poet; (f) writing poetry isn't work.)
- Activity 6. Students reflect on the Chairman's style of speech. (Answer: matter of fact, forceful, in control, lots of short sentences, no room for disagreement. It's a monologue.)
- Activity 7. Analysis of the poem. (Answer: eleven three-line verses; no rhyme/chime; variable line length; verses end-stopped; in-verse enjambment.)

Plenary (5 minutes): Ask students to classify the poem, expecting/eliciting that it's 'light verse', yet with a serious line to push that poetry-writing *is* a worthwhile job.

Homework: Students choose a job that they don't like and write a monologue (either prose or poetry) to the imaginary holder of that job, saying why it isn't worthwhile.

TASK SHEET: **That isn't a real job!**

1. What do you think about people who are writers, in general, and poets in particular? Is being a writer and poet a good job? Are they valuable to society? Discuss your ideas in groups of four.

2. Read the poem 'What the Chairman Told Tom' by Basil Bunting.

3. What facts can you find out, and what else can you imagine about the people mentioned in the poem? Complete the table.

Person	Known facts	Supposed details
The Chairman		
Mr Shaw		
Nancy		
Mr Hines		
Tom		

Compare your ideas with a partner.

4. What has Tom just done, and what is the Chairman doing in this poem?

5. What is the implication of
    a) what the Chairman says in verse 3 ?
    b) what the Chairman says in verse 5 ?
    c) what the Chairman says in verse 7 ?
    d) *My ten year old/can do it and rhyme* ?
    e) *I want to wash when I meet a poet* ?
    f) *Go and find work* ?
    Check your answers with a partner.

6. How would you describe the style and tone of the poem? What sort of person do you think the speaker (the Chairman) is?

7. Describe the structure of the poem.

8. Write a monologue to the holder of a job which you don't like and think is worthless, saying what you don't like about it and why you think it has no value. You can write it as a continuous paragraph of prose, or as a poem.

Advice on getting a good job

Introduction: In this lesson students will write a handout intended for other students about the process of getting a good job.

Aims and outcomes
- Students will write an audience-focussed handout about a process

Resources required: None.

Lesson starter (10 minutes): Ask students what their idea of a 'good job' is and list some of these qualities on the board (e.g. one with security, prospects for advancement, pension scheme, opportunities for leave for further training, pay and holiday conditions, location, hours . . .)

Main lesson (40 minutes)
- Give out the task sheet and ask students to get into groups of four to complete the table in Activity 1.
- Call back ideas from the whole class, and make a master list on the board for everyone to refer to. (Possible answers: you need to have: qualifications/some work experience/a presentable appearance/a good attitude/a curriculum vitae (CV); you need to: get in touch with different companies/talk to people who know about that sort of work/read things on the internet/read books about it ; you need to know: what that sector of work is like/what the prospects are for the future/where you want to be in ten years time/why you want to do that kind of work)
- Tell students that they are going to produce a practical A4 (one side) handout which will help students prepare for getting a good job, by offering useful tips.
- Ask them to plan their handout using the grid in Activity 3 for note-making.

Plenary (10 minutes): When students come to actually write the handout, point them to the language in Activity 4 which will help them structure what they write.

Homework (this will require extra time afterwards, in a second lesson): Ask students to produce their first draft for homework.
- When they have finished their first draft, put them together with two other pairs to read each other's first drafts and comment on the organization and layout, and offer suggestions about how they might improve it; also, if they notice any language errors (e.g. bad spelling, wrong tenses) they should underline the errors and leave them for the authors to correct.
- They should then produce a second draft taking the comments into account, and hand it in for you to see.

TASK SHEET: **Advice on getting a good job**

1. Get into a group of four and discuss how a student should go about getting a good job. Use the table below to organize your discussion.

In order to get a good job after school		
You need to have	You need to do	You need to know

2. Now work in a pair. You are going to design a one-page A4-size handout for students which will give them the information they need for getting a good job.

3. The information will need to be clear and simply written, and presented in an organized and accessible way. You could divide it into sections as in Activity 1, or think of your own way of organizing it. Use the framework below to plan a rough version of your handout.

TITLE:

Section 1

Section 2

Section 3

Summary/Conclusion

4. Use suitable structures to organize the advice: *It's a good idea if you . . . you must/should/ought to . . . you mustn't/shouldn't/ought not to . . . try to . . . you will make a better impression if you . . . make sure you do/don't . . . don't forget to . . . remember to . . .*

Section 3   Wild Things

Room for all of us?

Introduction: This lesson gives a chance to explore a classic modernist poem by D. H. Lawrence ('Mountain Lion') and also look at the moral issues it raises. There is also cross-text work with a passage of factual information about Mountain Lions.

Aims and outcomes

- To read and understand a modernist poem by a classic British author
- To discuss issues of man's attitudes to animals
- To do some creative writing

Resources required: You will need a copy of D H Lawrence's poem 'Mountain Lion'. Which you can find on the following websites:

> www.bravebirds.org/lawrence1.html
> www.eteaching-austria.at/02_cont/03content/03_englisch/eng_pp/poetry/mountain_lion.html

For additional material *see* the website.

Lesson starter (10 minutes): Ask students in pairs to list as many different wild members of the cat family as they can, also saying where they are found (e.g. tiger – India/elsewhere; lion – Africa; leopard – Africa; cheetah – Africa; wild cat – Britain/Europe; lynx – Spain/Europe; jaguar – South America). If they don't mention mountain lion (cougar/puma) then try to elicit it through questions: 'What about North America?' 'Have you ever seen a big cat in a western film?' You can ask for any other facts they know about each species (e.g. colour, size, prey, habitat). Ask what the situation of many of these species is, and why? (Answer: endangered, because of man using their space and killing them.)

Main lesson (40 minutes)

- Give students the task sheet and ask them to read the text in Activity 1, and then answer the questions in Activity 2 individually; they can then check with a partner. Call back the answers from the whole class. (Answers: (a) it is found in many different places over a very wide area; (b) it has a single colour with no patterns; (c) it lives by itself; (d) it hunts by hiding and jumping out on its prey; (e) it preys on other animals and eats meat; (f) it has been killed by people to the extent that it is now absent in places where it once lived; (g) it does most things at night.
- Give out/display the Lawrence poem and ask students to read it.
- Ask them to do Activity 4 individually, then check with a partner; then call back the answers – you can list them on the board. (Answers (Lawrence's words first): *spruce-trees – pine forests; Lobo Valley/Sangre de Cristo mountains/Picoris – Mexico; canyon – canyon yellow – sandy; mountain lion – mountain lion; cat – wild cat; stripes – light stripes; lair – lair; hole – cave; rocks – rocks; leap – leap*)
- Ask students to read the poem again and answer the questions. (Answers: (a) nervous – they are strangers, they have a gun, and men are to be feared; (b) 'foolish' – the Mexican knows he shouldn't have killed it, and Lawrence doesn't know what the laws are in Mexico; (c) he gives an intense sense of the beauty in the Mountain Lion's face, emphasising this with *bright, brilliant, sharp, fine, frost, keen* – all positive adjectives, plus the repetition of the same words; (d) he feels sad at her unnecessary death, and feels that it would be worth sacrificing a lot of people for one wild cat.

(continued on page 58)

TASK SHEET: **Room for all of us?**

1. Read the information below.

Mountain Lion (puma concolor)

The mountain lion is the most widespread animal in the Americas, living from northern British Columbia right down to Tierra del Fuego. It is as much at home in pine forests at 4,000 metres as it is in the Florida Everglades, the Sonora Desert in Arizona and the tropical jungles of Mexico. Because of this enormous range, six subspecies have been identified, and they also have many other names, depending where they are found: cougar, panther, painter, puma and catamount are some of the 40 names that have been noted. Their favoured habitat is steep rock canyon country.

Adult male mountain lions are around 2.4 metres long from nose to tail, and average 62 kg in weight, standing around 70 cm at the shoulder. This makes it the fourth biggest wild cat in the world, after tigers, lions and leopards. The females are smaller. As the Latin name *concolor* suggests, they have one colour, which can be sandy, grey or tawny. They have clear yellow eyes, sometimes with light stripes around the face and a pink nose.

The animals are solitary, except at mating time, and the females raise the two or three cubs alone for around 20 months after birth. They are also secretive animals, preferring to hunt at night, when they ambush animals such as deer and wild goats. They also take smaller animals such as rabbits, birds, and even insects. Because of their hunting technique they are able to leap from standing up to 5.5 metres in the air, and up to 12 metres in length. They can run at between 55 and 72 kmph over short distances. By day they lie up in a lair, which can be a cave in the rocks, or other similar hidden place.

Unfortunately, like many large predators, they have been hunted to extinction in many areas of the Americas, and they are now protected throughout their range. They will take domestic animals such as horses, cows and sheep, which makes them unpopular with farmers, though they rarely attack humans, largely because of their nocturnal habits and the wild places in which they live.

2. What do these words and phrases tell us about the mountain lion?
   a) *enormous range*   d) *ambush*   f) *hunted to extinction*
   b) *concolor*   e) *predator*   g) *nocturnal habits*
   c) *solitary*

3. Read D. H. Lawrence's poem 'Mountain Lion', which he wrote in Mexico

4. What connections – in either the actual words, synonyms or the ideas – can you find between Lawrence's poem and the passage in Activity 1?

5. Read the poem again and answer these questions:
   (a) How does he feel initially when they meet the two men, and why?
   (b) How does the Mexican feel on being found with the dead Mountain Lion, and how does Lawrence feel?
   (c) What impressions does he give about the Mountain Lion in the two parts where he describes it? (*Lift up her face* to *beautiful dead eyes*) And how does he do that?
   (d) At the end, how does he feel about the Mountain Lion's death?

6. Do you agree with Lawrence's ideas about the Mountain Lion and people? Talk to a partner and explain your reasons why/why not.

7. What do you notice about Lawrence's use of language in this poem? What techniques does he use to make his points?

8. What other animals do you know which are being 'hunted to extinction' by humans, and are now endangered species? How can we resolve the situation? Discuss your ideas in a group of four.

- Activity 6 asks the students to examine Lawrence's statement, and decide whether they agree or not, and then state their position and back it up with reasons. Try to develop this into a whole-class discussion.
- In Activity 7, students reread the poem to analyse its language; they have already done this with two sections in Activity 5c. (Answers: the language is mostly very simple, very factual. He gives us an accurate picture of the place – its physical characteristics and its atmosphere. He uses repetition a lot to emphasize and build the picture. The end of the poem is in direct contrast to this, although equally simply put, in that it is what *I think* rather than factual detail.)
- Activity 8 asks students to expand on the Lesson starter, and think about the situation of big cats around the world, using their own knowledge from TV programmes, websites and newspapers. They should then pool their information in a group of four, and report back to the whole class.

Plenary (10 minutes): Expand the discussion begun in Activity 8, adding facts and information which you know about.

Homework: Ask the students to do a piece of writing, talking about the situation in the poem, using the detail from it for the background, but written *either* from the point of view of the Mexican who killed the Mountain Lion, *or* from the point of view of the Mountain Lion herself. 150 words. Encourage them to read each other's work when they have done it.

Differentiation: Allow for different students' knowledge of and interest in wild cats; however, the discussion about extinction should unite them as it is a global issue. The homework allows for two radically different points of view to be expressed. Anyone who has an idea for another 'voice' should be encouraged to use it (e.g. a game warden who meets the Mexicans further down the valley; the Mexican's wife when he gets the mountain lion home).

Danger!

Introduction: In this lesson, students read a first-hand account of a meeting with a mountain lion; they analyse the text for language and style, and do a role-play based on it.

Aims and outcomes

- To read and analyse a factual account
- To role-play a situation based on the account

Resources required: You need the article 'I fought off a mountain lion' by Lila Lifely from *The Guardian Weekend* magazine (06.06.2009), which you can find at:

 www.guardian.co.uk/lifeandstyle/2009/jun/06/experience-mountain-lion

Lesson starter (10 minutes): Ask students what they think happens when human beings meet big cats. Ask what humans should/can do in such situations.

Main lesson (40 minutes)

- Give students the text and ask students for the answers immediately after reading it. (Answers: (a) on Vancouver Island in Canada; (b) she was preparing dinner for a group of ten-year-old girls she had taken camping; (c) she hit it in the face with a stick; (d) she climbed a tree and shouted for help from another camping group; (d) she had surgery, and later married and had children.)
- Activity 3 gives students an opportunity to express their personal reactions to the incident.
- Activity 4. This could be a dictionary activity. (Answers: (a) a domestic cat that has become wild and aggressive; (b) to attack, cutting and battering the victim; (c) someone who is walking along and not paying attention; (d) a sound between a low noise of fear and the letting out of breath; (e) cut off something in a straight line; (f) having a plan which was not carefully thought through; (g) the mountain lion was only doing what was natural; (h) to decide whether to run away or stay and fight the 'enemy'.
- Students can decide what they find similar; possible answers: 'The peak had trees and shrubs on one side and bald rock on the other' is similar to Lawrence's description of the Lobo Valley; 'the mountain lion that springs from the rock face' is similar to 'So, she will never leap that way again with the yellow flash of a mountain lion's long shoot!'; 'It was beautiful: 8ft long, sleek and tan. I felt awful' resembles Lawrence's description of the Mountain Lion, and his feelings on seeing it dead.
- Activity 6. Text analysis. (Answers: It's a personal adventure story (from a newspaper section about people's unusual experiences); from a newspaper's Saturday magazine; to tell an exciting, unusual experience; it's told dramatically, mixing action, the writer's thoughts, and accessible, straightforward speech; it's well told, because it engages and holds attention.)
- Activity 7. A role play, giving the 'Lila' student the chance to retell the story, and the 'police officer' to ask questions and make notes. Suggest they ask for details not given in the story (e.g. how many girls were in the group?) and make up suitable answers. Afterwards, they can change partners and switch roles.

Plenary (10 minutes): Ask students if they or anyone they know well has ever been in a dangerous situation of any kind; if so, have them tell the rest of the class about it. If not, have a story ready to tell them, either based on something that happened to you or someone you know, or something you have read.

Differentiation: Students are given several opportunities to react to the story – both through the questions, and through the role play in a personal and individual way.

TASK SHEET: **Danger!**

1. Read the text 'I fought off a mountain lion'.

2. Answer the following questions about the text:
   a) Where did this incident take place?
   b) What was Lila Lifely doing when it happened?
   c) How did she drive the mountain lion away?
   d) How did she get help?
   e) What happened to Alyson?

3. Think about what happened and decide:
   a) Do you think she did the right things in the situation?
   b) Could/would you have done these things, or something else?
   c) Do you think she deserved the Star of Courage medal? Why/why not?
   Talk to a partner and exchange ideas.

4. Explain the phrases in italics:
   a) 'the image in my head was of *a house cat gone feral.*'
   b) '"*It's mauling* Alyson.'"
   c) 'the mountain lion that springs from the rock face on to *the unwary passerby*'
   d) 'I heard a sound *halfway between a moan and an exhalation*'
   e) 'one side *had been sheared clean away* from the bone'
   f) '*harbouring an ill-conceived plan* to jump down and ambush the cougar'
   g) '*the cat hadn't been at fault*'
   h) 'choose "*fight*" over "*flight*"'
   Discuss your answers with a partner.

5. Can you find any *echoes* of the D. H. Lawrence poem 'Mountain Lion' which you read in lesson 3.1?

6. What kind of text is this? Where do you think it came from? What is its purpose? What style of language is used? Is the story well told – why/why not?

7. Role play. Work with a partner. One of you is Lila Lifely, the other is a police officer. Lila should make her statement to the police officer, saying what happened. The police officer should make notes and ask questions for clarification.

At the zoo

* Please note that this lesson should take approximately 1 hour and 40 minutes, so please use a double lesson or spread over 2 lessons.

Introduction: Students analyse the classic Ted Hughes poem 'The Jaguar', and also discuss their attitudes to zoos particularly through the final debate, which will run into a second lesson.

Aims and outcomes
* Close analysis of a contemporary poem
* Discussion of the ethical issues of keeping animals in zoos

Resources required: You will need a copy of 'The Jaguar' from its original source: Ted Hughes, *The Hawk in the Rain*. London: Faber, 1957, or from the recent (2005) Ted Hughes, *Collected Poems*. London: Faber. You can find it on the internet at:

www.geoffbarton.co.uk/files/student-resources/GCSE/the%20Jaguar.doc

Lesson starter (15 minutes): Ask the class about their experiences with zoos: which ones they have visited; when they last went; what it was like. Include safari and wildlife parks in the discussion, but not nature reserves.

Main lesson (45 minutes)
* Move on from the Lesson starter into Activity 1, getting the students to discuss the points raised in pairs. Suggest they note down their ideas for future reference. Open the discussion up to the whole class; it would be a good idea to list the pros and cons they give on the board.
* Ask them call out what they know about jaguars in a whole-class setting. (A large spotted cat, inhabiting dense jungles from Mexico south to northern Argentina; varies in size in different parts of its range from 56–96kg, adult length 1.62–1.83 m + 75 cm tail, stands 67–76 cm; predator taking a wide range of animals; strongest bite of all big cats; black form, know as a panther.)
* Ask students to read the poem, then answer the questions in Activity 4 (apes, fleas!), parrots, boa constrictor, tiger, lion) and 5. (Answers: (a) they are mostly asleep, because it's hot and sunny; (b) they are noisy and moving; (c) the jaguar, because he's walking up and down in his cage). They can check their answers with a partner before you ask for answers from the whole class.
* Activity 6 asks the students to look at particular pieces of language use. Again, they can do this individually before checking with a partner. (Answers: (a) you would literally shriek if you were on fire, but the parrots are probably red, yellow and orange, so look like fire, too; (b) everything is so still it looks like a painting of a zoo which might be in a child's room; (c) like a child who has woken up from an amazing dream and is standing still remembering the details; (d) a fortune-teller or prophet sees the future regardless of the room he is in.
* This activity asks students to analyse the structure of the poem. (Answer: it has five four-line verses. Each verse has a rhyme/pararhyme/chime scheme ABBA (verses 1/2/3/4) although verse 3 is less precise than the others, ABAB (verse 5). Each line is around 10 syllables long, with 9, 11, 12 occurring.)
* Activity 8 asks students to look for examples of literary techniques. (Answers: (a) *as if they were on fire; like cheap tarts; still as the sun; as a child at a dream;* (b) *the boa constrictor's coil is a fossil;* (c) *still as the sun; stinks of sleeps . . . straw* (all these /s/ sounds sound like sleeping);

(continued on page 64)   62

TASK SHEET: **At the zoo**

1. What do you think of zoos? Are they good or bad things for people? Are they good or bad things for the animals? Discuss your ideas with a partner, making sure you back up your ideas with arguments.

2. What do you know about Jaguars? Where are they from? What do they look like? What are their habits?

3. Read the poem 'The Jaguar' by Ted Hughes.

4. List the creatures that are mentioned at Hughes's zoo.

5. Answer these questions about the content of the poem:
   a) What is the state of most animals at the zoo? Why do you think they are like this?
   b) How are the parrots different to the other creatures?
   c) What is everyone watching, and why?

6. Look at these particular pieces of language; why does Hughes use them?
   a) 'The parrots shriek *as if they were on fire.*'
   b) '*It might be painted on a nursery wall.*'
   c) 'stares, *mesmerized, / like a child at a dream,*'
   d) '*more than to the visionary his cell*'
   Discuss you answers with a partner.

7. Now read the poem again and work out the structure of it.

8. Find as many examples of these things as you can:
   a) simile
   b) metaphor
   c) alliteration
   d) enjambement
   Compare your answers with a partner.

9. What difference in tone do you find between the first two verses and the last three?

10. Do you think Hughes is right about the jaguar's feelings?

runs like the rest . . . arrives (the /r/ sound of activity); *fierce fuse* (the /f/ sound fizzes); *bang of blood in the brain* (the /b/ sound hits us); (d) from verse 1 to 2; verse 3 to 4; verse 4 to 5.
- This activity asks students to be sensitive to the tone created by the language used. The first two verses are quiet and sleepy (e.g. *yawn and adore; fatigued with indolence*). From the 'But' of verse 3 there is an urgency (*jaguar hurrying enraged; his stride is wildernesses of freedom*).
- In Activity 10, students can decide if they agree with Hughes's idea that the jaguar is not pacing its cage because it is bored (as people often think), but because it is elsewhere, imagining itself free in the wild.

Plenary (40 minutes): Follow this up with a debate: 'This House Believes that Zoos are Bad for Animals'. Invite/select two speakers for and against; while they prepare ask the other students to make a set of three questions they can put to each side – they can do this in pairs.

Homework: Ask students to write 100–150 words on their opinion about why zoos are good or bad for animals and people.

Differentiation: The activities allow students to express different opinions about the place of zoos in society.

Dinner time!

Introduction: In this lesson, students read a text related to the zoo theme of lesson 3.3, and analyse the way it's structured, and the language used, and construct their own sentences based on it.

Aims and outcomes
- To read a prose passage closely and analyse its structure and language
- To use the language found to make their own sentences

Resources required: The extract from Gerald Durrell (1972) *Catch Me A Colobus*. London: Collins. *See* the website for additional related materials (Resource Bank).

Lesson starter (10 minutes): Ask students whether they have any pets and what they feed them on. Discuss the options with them (e.g. canned food, real meat, bones, biscuits for dogs).

Main lesson (45 minutes)
- Activity 1: Discuss what problems might occur and how they might be solved (e.g. getting live food for snakes, and food for animals that only eat one thing).
- Activity 3. Give out the text. Students read, write and compare their summaries. (Possible answer: the author discusses the difficulty of feeding wild animals in captivity, describing the feeding of a pangolin, and suggesting the need for a cookery book.)
- Activity 4. Idiomatic animal phrases. Students link an animal to a key word, write the whole phrase, then say what it means. Decide on dictionary use. (Answers: to have a bee in one's bonnet (to be concerned about something obsessively); birds of a feather (people of the same kind); a black sheep (an outcast); like a red rag to a bull (something which angers someone); butterflies in one's stomach (nervousness); no room to swing a cat (a very small space); a dark horse (someone who keeps quiet about something); a fly in the ointment (a problem); a dog's dinner (a mess); a white elephant (something useless, or which causes trouble).
- Activity 5 looks at the vocabulary in some of the more complicated phrases. (Answers: (a) begin to show all their strange behaviours to increase your knowledge; (b) do what they want, in the same way that you would let an old woman with a small dog do what she wanted; (c) these strange animals which look like a moving fir cone with tails.)
- Activity 6. Works on the structure of content. (Answers: para 1: general problems of feeding wild animals in captivity; para 2: problems of feeding the pangolin; para 3: a recipe by a TV cook; para 4: reflections on writing a book of recipes for animal.)
- Activity 7 asks students to work on connectors for linking ideas in sentences, using three examples from the passage to make their own sentences. (Example answers: It's one thing to do a practice exam in class, but it's a different kettle of fish when you take the real exam. One day they say he's the best player in the team and the next day they say he's rubbish. But unless you behave nicely to them, they will not let you play there when you want to.)
- Activity 8 works on style and purpose. (Answer: the amusement comes partly from his description of the animals behaviour related to food, his description of the pangolin itself, but mostly from his imitation of a TV cook, and the idea of writing the recipe book.)

Plenary (5 minutes): Ask students to comment on whether they think a book of recipes for animals is a viable proposition, and say why or why not.

Homework: Ask students to write two recipes for unusual animals.

Differentiation: Students have the opportunity to produce work at their own level and reflecting their own interests in Activity 7, and for homework.

TASK SHEET: Dinner time!

1. What do animals get fed on when they're in a zoo? Think about what different animals feed on in the wild, and what they might be given in captivity. Talk to a partner about it.

2. Read the text.

3. Summarize the content in one sentence of not more than 25 words.

4. In the first sentence the author uses the idiomatic phrase 'a different kettle of fish', which means 'a completely different situation'. Match the animals with a partner word that goes with it make an idiomatic phrase, write the whole phrase and then explain the meaning of each phrase.

bee	bird	sheep	bull	butterflies	cat	horse	fly	dog	elephant
dinner	bonnet	feather	white	ointment	red rag	black	dark	stomach	swing

Compare your answers with a partner's.

5. Explain the meaning of some of the author's original phrases:
   a) 'start exhibiting all their eccentricities for your edification'
   b) 'indulge them, as you would indulge an elderly lady with her pekinese'
   c) 'these curious beasts that look like animated fir cones with tails'

6. How is this text structured? Make brief notes about what the four paragraphs are about

Paragraph 1

....

Paragraph 2

....

Paragraph 3

....

Paragraph 4

....

7. Look at the way the writer structures his sentences in the first paragraph, using different connecting phrases:

   > Sentence 1: 'It's one thing to . . . but it's a different kettle of fish when . . .'
   > Sentences 3–4: 'One day they . . . The next day they . . .'
   > Sentence 5: 'But unless you . . . they will not . . .'

   Use these connecting phrases to make three sentences of your own, on topics of your own choice.

8. The text is a piece of humorous writing. Where does the humour come from?

One for sorrow

Introduction: Students will read a different style of poem – about a magpie – and then write a similar poem of their own about another bird/animal.

Aims and outcomes

- Students will read about a magpie and examine traditional attitudes to the species.
- They will analyse the poem, then write a similar poem of their own.

Resources required: The poem 'Magpie' from Esther Morgan (2001) *Beyond Calling Distance*. Tarset: Bloodaxe Books.

Lesson starter (5 minutes): Ask students if they can complete the 'One for sorrow' traditional rhyme (One for sorrow/Two for joy/Three for a girl/Four for a boy/Five for silver/Six for gold/Seven for a story never to be told) and ask them what it's about (fortune-telling through the number of magpies you see together).

Main lesson (50 minutes)

- Hand out the task sheet and ask students to do Activity 1. Once the groups have compared notes, call back ideas from the whole class; you may want to note them on the board under various headings (e.g. Appearance/Food/Habits) for later reference.
- Hand out/display the poem 'Magpie' by Esther Morgan, and ask students to read it.
- Ask them to examine the content and complete the table. (Answers: verse 1 / lines 1–7 are about the bird's appearance: portrayed as a *mobster* and someone in a tuxedo; verse 1 / lines 8–13 are about what it eats, mentioning stealing other birds' eggs, and human's top-of-the-milk; verse 2 about stealing shiny objects; also, strangely, our words; verse 3 the meeting with the bird on the road; its behaviour; her reaction.)
- Activity 5 asks students to explain particularly unusual bits of language/ideas. They are all open to personal interpretation. (Possible answers: (a) perhaps that the 'jewels' the bird collects are riches on which to build future dreams; (b) this perhaps implies it would steal anything valuable if it could [the use of the conditional tense means it isn't given the chance – 'you'd do it if you could']; (c) the magpie seems to be deciding if the author would make a good meal or not; (d) the magpie is seen as a symbol of bad luck; she salutes the bird in a kind of respect, maybe to ward off the evil.)
- In Activity 6 students analyse the poem's structure. (Answer: the poem has three verses, each of 13 lines (maybe related to the 'bad luck' associated with the subject bird?); it has no rhyme, or regular number of syllables per line, varying from 2–7, with 4/5 syllables being most frequent. It is a 'long, thin' poem!)
- Students look at a particular poetic technique which is used clearly. (Answers: the magpie is personified as a mafia 'mobster', a diner dressed in dinner jacket.)

Plenary (5 minutes): Ask students for opinions on the poem, whether it's a good portrayal of the bird, whether they might have added anything else (e.g. its cackling voice, that it 'murders' baby birds).

Homework: Ask students to write their own 'long, thin' poem for homework, about another (common) creature they know about. Discuss the fox example with them.

Differentiation: Students will have varying degrees of knowledge about magpies (although there are frequently campaigns against and for them in the British press), and also about other animals. If they want to choose a pet they know, rather than a wild animal or bird, and find suitable metaphors and characteristics for that, then let them do that.

TASK SHEET: **One for sorrow**

1. What do you know about magpies? What do they look like? Where do they live? What do they eat? How are they viewed by people? Share your ideas in a group of four.

2. Read the poem 'Magpie' by Esther Morgan.

3. Did you find anything in the poem that was the same as or similar to what your group discussed?

4. Look at how the poet organizes her poem. What does she talk about in each of these sections, and what details does she tell us about the magpie in them? Complete the table below with the information:

Section	Topic	Details
Verse 1, lines 1–7		
Verse 1, lines 8–13		
Verse 2		
Verse 3		

Compare your table with a partner's.

5. What do you understand by the following:
   a) *Dream-hoarder* (verse 2, line 3)
   b) *You'd nick . . .*
      the words right out
      of our gaping mouths (verse 2, lines 11–13)
   c) *You eye me up*
      as I drive past. (verse 3, lines 10–11)
   d) *Bad luck.*
      I salute you. (verse 3, lines 12–13)

6. Analyse the structure of this poem.

7. What examples of personification are there in the poem?

8. Think about another bird or animal to which people traditionally give certain attributes (e.g. the fox – think about Aesop's fable about the fox and the crow, Roald Dahl's story *Fantastic Mr Fox*, the fox in the *Chicken Licken* story). Write your own 'long thin' poem about it.

Dog turns wolf

Introduction: This extract is from the very end of the story where the protagonist sledge-dog Buck goes off into the wild with the timber wolf pack – something he's been moving towards throughout the story.

Aims and outcomes

- To read an extract from a famous American story, where a dog is the protagonist
- To analyse the structure of the extract and the writer's style

Resources required: Paragraphs 9–5 from the end of Chapter 7 'The Sounding of the Call' from Jack London (1903/1992) *The Call of the Wild*. Ware: Wordsworth Classics. It is also available online at:

 http://london.sonoma.edu/Writings/CallOfTheWild/chapter7.html

Lesson starter (10 minutes): Ask the class who has a dog, or sees a dog (e.g. a relative's or a neighbour's) regularly. Ask in what ways they think dogs behave like wild animals. (e.g. scenting, listening, barking/urinating for territory, attacking, snarling . . .)

Main lesson (40 minutes)

- Give out the task sheets and ask students to do Activity 1 in a group of four. Call back answers from the whole class. You might want to list ideas on the board.
- Hand out/display the extract from Jack London's *The Call of the Wild* for students to read.
- Ask them to complete the table in Activity 3 individually, then compare their answers with a partner. (Answers: (1) Buck senses and hears the arrival of the wolf pack; (2) the wolves arrive and some attack, but Buck fights them off; (3) the whole pack attack, and Buck retreats to the safety of a corner to protect his back; (4) he continues to fight them off, and eventually a wolf he had already met greets him; (5) an older wolf also greets him, all the wolves howl, and Buck joins in, and the pack leaves with Buck.)
- Activity 4 asks students to analyse the core of the extract, indeed the whole story. (Answer: they show Buck reacting some primitive instinct inside him, when he hears the wolves yelp and howl – it is 'the call of the wild' – and he wants to be part of that.)
- Activity 5 asks for analysis of the key action of the extract. (Answer: he has to fight to prove his strength, and then he is accepted; then they howl together, and leave together.)
- Activity 6 looks at the quality of London's descriptive writing to conjure the scene. (Possible answers: *lighting the land till it lay bathed in ghostly day; Into the clearing where the moonlight streamed, they poured in a silvery flood.*)

Plenary (10 minutes): Bring the discussion full circle, and get students to discuss whether there is a 'call of the wild' for domestic animals, and ask for examples.

Homework: Ask students to research online to find out where Buck came from (California) and how he became a sledge-dog in the Klondike (he was stolen, and sold, broken, and transported, along with hundreds of other dogs).

Differentiation: This lesson offers students with dogs or who know dogs well to contribute a lot to the discussions.

TASK SHEET: Dog turns wolf

1. What do you know about wolves? Work in a group of four and pool your information.

2. Read the extract from Jack London's *The Call of the Wild*.

3. Complete the table below with brief notes about the main action in each of the five paragraphs:

Paragraph	Main action
1	
2	
3	
4	
5	

Compare your table with a partner's.

4. Look at these two sentences:

   'Again Buck knew them as things heard in that other world which persisted in his memory.'

   'And now the call came to Buck in unmistakable accents.'

   What is Buck listening to? And what do you understand by 'that other world which persisted in his memory'? Discuss your ideas with your partner.

5. What does Buck have to do before he is accepted by the wolves, and what happens when he is accepted?

6. Apart from describing Buck and the wolves very accurately, London also describes the scene in which the action takes place. Find examples of poetic descriptions of this scene.

Understanding geese

Introduction: This lesson introduces students to a poem in a regional variety of English – Scots, so that they have to cope not just with the poetical ideas, but also language which they may find unfamiliar.

Aims and outcomes

- Students will encounter a poem written in the language of one of the varieties of English from the British Isles

Resources required: The poem 'Skeins o geese' from Kathleen Jamie (1994) *The Queen of Sheba*. Newcastle-upon-Tyne: Bloodaxe Books. It can be found online at:

 www.versedaily.org/skeinogeese.shtml

Lesson starter (10 minutes): Ask students what they know about birds and migration. Expect answers regarding summer visitors to the UK which fly south in the winter, to Africa (e.g. swallows, cuckoos, various species of warbler), and birds which breed in the north – Scandinavia, Russia, Greenland, Iceland – and migrate south to winter in the UK (e.g. various species of geese, various species of wader).

Main lesson (35 minutes)

- Give out the task sheets and ask students to get into groups of four to pool their knowledge about wild geese. Call back the information they give you and make notes on the board. If they don't give you details about them flying in V-formation skeins, try to elicit some. Make sure they understand *skeins* and the shapes flying geese make, as it's central to the poem's meanings.
- Hand out/display the poem 'Skeins o geese' by Kathleen Jamie, and ask students to read it.
- Plainly, the reaction to Activities 2 and 3 will vary depending on whether you are working with Scots-speaking students or not. If you are working with Scots speakers, then skip Activity 3. (Answers: it is non-standard English. It is Scots. Individual reactions to it will vary.)
- Activity 4 aims to open up what might at first seem 'difficult', and show how easy it is to understand with a little thought. (Answers: (a) of; (b) like; (c) before; (d) was; (e) lowing – not a common word except in Christmas carols – *the cattle are lowing, the baby awakes*!)
- Activity 5 asks students to work through the poem, working out what the Scots words are in Standard English (*see* the 'translation' of the whole poem in the Resource Bank).
- Activity 6 asks students to look at figures of speech: the central metaphor of the poem, and some similes. (Answers: metaphor she says the form of the skeins, and broken skeins, are writing; the similes: verse 1: the sky is full of geese moving, and honking, which she says is like cattle lowing; verse 3: the barbed wire looks like some old sort of writing (runic, perhaps).)
- This is quite a complicated reference pattern, because the first four lines of verse 4 are commenting on what she says in verse 3 about not understanding the words the geese and the wire make (the three things she mentions are things she does understand and can communicate with). (Answer: the way the geese's noise recedes into the distance (beautiful poetic image – 'the hem of its going'!) – *its* refers to *the word* in verse 3, which whistles away without her understanding it.)
- Activity 9 asks students to analyse the formal aspects of the poem. (Answer: The poem has five five-line verses, with no rhyme/chime scheme; the lines vary from four to eleven syllables, with seven syllables being most frequent; the verses are end-stopped, but there is in-verse enjambment; intial capitalization only occurs where there is a new sentence).

(continued on page 74)

TASK SHEET: **Understanding geese**

1. Work in a group of four. Pool all your knowledge about wild geese.

2. Read the poem 'Skeins o geese' by Kathleen Jamie.

3. What do you notice about the language it is written in? What is it? What is your reaction to it?

4. Look at these words from verse 1. How would you write them in standard British English?
   a) *o* _____   d) *wis* _____
   b) *lik* _____   e) *lowin* _____
   c) *afore* _____

5. Now work with a partner, and go through the other verses and work out what other words are in Standard British English.

6. What metaphor does the poet use about what the geese do? (*see* verses 1 and 5) Find examples of a similes in verses 1 and 3 – what is their effect?

7. In verse 2 she says she's 'blin/tae a' soon but geese ca'ing'. Why is this a strange image, and what does she mean?

8. What does 'The hem of its goin drags across the sky' mean? What does *its* refer back to?

9. Analyse the formal structure of the poem.

10. What is the poet trying to do in this poem? Do you think she succeeds? Explain why/why not.

11. Kathleen Jamie writes both in Standard English and in Scots. Why do you think she chose to write this particular poem in Scots rather than Standard English?

12. 'The poem "Skeins o geese" is patterned on sound.' Explain this statement, and illustrate your answer. Write 200 words on a separate piece of paper.

Plenary (15 minutes)

- Students will need to look at the final verse carefully to understand the full meaning of the poem. (Answer: she wants to understand the geese, and what they 'mean' – she feels the forms they 'write' in the sky and the noise they make must hold something that can be communicated; she finds the human past, death and relationships (verse 3) easy to understand, but these wild things are difficult, and she is left with sounds – the geese, the wind, which are 'maybe human' – but which she is deprived of (the use of the adjective 'bereft' in this way is very unusual!). So perhaps she is saying that the natural world is its own world, and we can understand our human world, but will not be able to read the 'messages' from nature.)

- This is a big question, and one that one perhaps needs the poet to answer! (Possible answer: as Kathleen Jamie is Scottish, maybe she feels more comfortable talking about such fundamental things as communicating with nature in a language that is closer to her. Plus, she presumably had this experience with the massive flocks of wintering geese somewhere on the Scottish coast, and so it was a 'Scottish' experience. Also, the form of Scots she uses here is much more easily accessible to Standard British English speakers than other forms that exist.)

Homework: An essential part of this poem is the patterning of sound; this is because a lot of the content is about not understanding the sound the geese make. The written homework focuses on this.

Differentiation: By examining a poem in another form of English, students will be helped towards attitudes of inclusion, and an understanding that we can all use our own version of the language and still belong.

Cats or dogs?

Introduction: This lesson deals with an interesting modern poem apparently about the undesirability of cats, but actually a clever attack on prejudice.

Aims and outcomes

- To have students read, enjoy and analyse a contemporary poem
- To explore the way that literature can work at different levels

Resources required: The poem 'Mort aux chats' from Peter Porter (1972) *Preaching to the Converted*. Oxford: Oxford University Press. It is also available online at:

 http://warlight.tripod.com/PPorter.html
www.clivejames.com/guest-poets/peter-porter/mort-aux-chats

Lesson starter (10 minutes): Ask students how many of them have cats, how many dogs, how many both. Ask how dogs and cats get on with each other, and why.

Main lesson (40 minutes)

- Give out the task sheets and ask students to do Activity 1 and share their feelings with a partner. Call back some ideas from the whole class. You might start a table on the board with four columns – Cats: Likes / Dislikes, Dogs: Likes / Dislikes – to collect their feelings in.
- Hand out/display the poem 'Mort aux chats' by Peter Porter WITHOUT the final two lines, and ask students to read it.
- Ask students to do Activities 3, 4 and 5 individually, then check with a partner. (Answers: 3: it is a list of things cats are supposed to do; it is supposed to turn people against cats – if they don't mention it, draw students' attention to the opening line. 4: some are ridiculous ('I blame my headache and my/plants dying on to cats'), some are untrue (cats consume seven times/ their own weight in food a week), some are based on false evidence ('Cats/sit down to pee (our scientists/have proved it)'); 5: students should speculate – the only 'outside' information comes from 'they stabbed us in the back/last time' and 'our scientists/have proved it'.)
- Activity 6 asks them to look at a piece of vocabulary, and then try to explain it. (Answers: it means to do something underhand to bring somebody down in some way; student speculation for the second part.)
- Activity 7 asks them to speculate on the missing final two lines. After pair discussion, elicit some ideas . . . then give them the last two lines. Congratulate anyone who was correct!
- Activity 8 analyses the formal structure of the poem. (Answer: it is 36 lines long, in free verse, with no rhyme/chime scheme; lines are from 5–11 syllables long, with 7 syllables most frequent; initial capitalization is only used for new sentences; lines run on.)

Plenary (10 minutes): Ask students to discuss the poem and suggest its purpose.

Homework: Ask them to write the essay for homework.

Differentiation: The homework gives everyone ample scope to deal with their experiences of racial prejudice.

TASK SHEET: **Cats or dogs?**

1. Which do you prefer, cats or dogs? Say what you like and dislike about each animal. Share your ideas with a partner.

2. Read the poem 'Mort aux chats' by Peter Porter. You have all except the last two lines. Think about the next three questions:

3. What is this poem? What is its object?

4. What do you think about the things that are said about cats?

5. Who do you think the *I* of the poem is? Compare your answers to questions 3–5 with a partner.

6. What does the expression *to stab someone in the back* mean? Look at lines 21–22. Who are *they* and who are *us*?

7. What do you imagine might be in the missing last two lines? Discuss your ideas with a partner.

8. Analyse the structure of the poem.

9. 'The poem "Mort aux chats" is actually an attack on racial prejudice.' Explain this statement, with reference to the poem (250 words).

Writing about keeping dogs

Introduction: This writing task can usefully follow on from lesson 3.8, where there was discussion about keeping dogs and cats.

Aims and outcomes
- Students plan and write a discursive essay on the topic given
- They carry out peer correction on their partner's essay

Resources required: None

Lesson starter (10 minutes): Ask where students think is the best place to keep a dog, and start a class discussion.

Main lesson (35 minutes)
- Give out the task sheets and have students brainstorm their ideas about keeping dogs in pairs; call back ideas from the whole class, and write them up on a master table on the board.
- Read out the title of the essay they're going to write, and ask them to decide individually what they believe, and whether they are going to argue for or against the statement.
- Ask them to plan out their essay, using the framework in Activity 3. Circulate and help with ideas and organization, if necessary.
- Point out the comment about language and examples in Activity 4. This is intended to set them on the right path; you may wish to elicit more examples of the kind of discourse markers they might use at the different stages of the essay.

Plenary (15 minutes)
- When they have finished, pair students for peer correction. Ask them to concentrate on the organization, and make suggestions to their partner about how they think it might be improved. If they notice any language errors (e.g. spelling, verb tense) then they can underline these in pencil and point them out to their partner, without telling them what they should be – the partner should self-correct.
- When they have finished the correction, ask them to write a second draft, which will be handed in to you for reading.

Homework
- Once they have planned their essay, ask them to either write a first draft in class or as homework.

Differentiation: The topic allows for all students to express their own opinions and ideas freely.

TASK SHEET: **Writing about keeping dogs**

1. Think about this issue: is it all right to keep a dog in flat or a town house? Write down notes on the advantages and disadvantages for the owners and the dog.

Keeping a dog in a flat or town house

ADVANTAGES   DISADVANTAGES

Compare and share your notes with a partner, and extend your lists.

2. You are now going to write an essay on the following topic: 'It is wrong to keep a dog in a flat or town house.' Discuss.
   - Decide whether you agree with the statement or not. This decides how you will organize your essay.
   - You will need to put forward neutral arguments for and against the statement, then make a conclusion expressing your own personal opinion.

3. Use the framework below to plan your essay out before you write it.

Introduction (state the issue that you are discussing)

....

Arguments for the title statement

....
....

Arguments against the title statement

....
....

Conclusion (including your personal view)

....
....
....
....

4. When you write, make sure that you organize your paragraphs carefully, with the right sort of language, e.g. *Many/some people believe/think that . . . on the other hand . . . in my opinion . . .*

Section 4   Family

A sister

Introduction: This first lesson in the Family section asks students to look at the rather strange story of a man who has invented an imaginary *little sister*.

Aims and outcomes
- To read and enjoy a contemporary poem about relationships
- To analyse the poem in terms of its content, and its structure

Resources required: The poem 'Little Sister' from J. C. Hall (1985) *Selected & New Poems 1939–84*. London: Secker & Warburg.

Lesson starter (15 minutes): Ask students to draw their family tree, and then tell a partner about the people in their family, saying who they are closest to, who they like and dislike and why.

Main lesson (35 minutes)
- Give out the task sheet and ask students to do Activity 1 individually, then talk to a partner about their ideas. Call back some comments from the whole class.
- Give out copies of the poem and ask students to read it. Ask them to answer the question in Activity 3 in a whole-class setting. (Answer: he reveals that the *little sister* doesn't exist.)
- Indicate that he calls the invented story a *history*, and ask students to do Activity 4 individually, then check their answers with a partner. (Answers: (a) their childhood until he was nine – sleeping arrangements and activities; (b) what happened in their teenage years; (c) her marriage. They were close as children, but grew apart as teenagers, but he seems to like her husband, although what he says about the photo suggests they don't see each other.)
- Ask the whole class to answer the question in Activity 5. (Answer: that he is unsure whether the photo of the woman is his sister.)
- Activity 5 has a question which is open to individual interpretation, but students should back their arguments for one or the other answer with facts from the text. (Answers: probably (b) or (c) – from 'a life couldn't achieve' – it sounds as if they tried and failed, either through miscarriage or infertility.)
- This activity examines the structure of the poem (Answer: five verses of 6 lines each, in an ABCABC rhyme/chime scheme (e.g. verse 1: *room-arm; dark-cheek; dress-distress*), although verse 4 moves to ABACBC. There are between 8 and 12 syllables per line, though mostly between 8 and 10.)
- Activity 8 asks students to look for any techniques used. (Answers: (a) no simile; (b) metaphor at the end of the verse 2, where the piano is *stumbling over its notes*, rather than the children playing it; (c) consonance in *shimmering she* in verse 5, which makes it sound hazy; (d) enjambement occurs between verse 3 and 4.)

Plenary (10 minutes): Activity 8 asks students to give a personal reaction to this poem, and what the author reveals about himself. Do this as a whole-class round-up of the work on the poem. (Possible answers: he's rather strange to maintain such an elaborate fiction as an adult; he must have been, and still be, very lonely, and so is to be pitied.)

Homework: Ask students to write a dialogue between the author and a psychologist, in which they examine the need for this fictional sister, and the author explains his reasons and feelings.

Differentiation: Make allowances in Activity 1 for the different experiences students have had with their siblings at home; there will probably be no consensus.

TASK SHEET: **A sister**

1. If you are a boy and have a sister, or a girl and have a brother, think what is good and what is bad about it. If you don't have a sibling of the opposite sex, what do you think would be good or bad about it? Make notes in the table below, then share your ideas with a partner.

Good things about having a sibling of the opposite sex	Bad things about having a sibling of the opposite sex

2. Read the poem called 'Little Sister' by J. C. Hall.

3. What is surprising about the end of the poem?

4. What stages of the *history* of the relationship are dealt with a) in verses 1 and 2? b) in verse 3? c) in verse 4? How does the relationship change over time? Discuss your answers with a partner.

5. What in verse 4 might give the reader a clue that there's something not right about this *history*?

6. What do you think is the truth about the *little sister*?
   a) she never existed and his parents never thought of having another child
   b) she died in his mother's womb the author's parents were unable to have other children though they wanted to
   Tell a partner, giving reasons for your decision based on what is said in the poem.

7. Examine the structure of the poem and say how it works.

8. Can you find any examples of these features in the poem?
   a) simile
   b) metaphor
   c) consonance
   d) verse enjambement

9. What are your feelings towards the author after this revelation?

Mother and daughter

Introduction: This lesson examines a difficult relationship between a mother and daughter.

Aims and outcomes
- To examine and discuss the portrayal of a mother-daughter relationship
- To analyse the language and content used by the poet to show the situation

Resources required: The poem 'Mother and Daughter in Bewley's Café' from Anne Haverty (1999) *The Beauty of the Moon*. London: Chatto & Windus (Resource Bank).

Lesson starter (10 minutes): Students reflect on their relationships with each of their parents, deciding how and why they are different. Extend this to a pair/whole class discussion as appropriate.

Main lesson (40 minutes)
- Give out the task sheet. This activity expands from the students' reflections in the lesson starter to concentrate only on girls' relationships with their parents. After the individual and group phases, invite whole-class discussion. You may want to make notes on the board.
- Activity 3. Students read the poem and answer. (Answers: (a) it feels like someone who is sitting in the café watching them, though an omniscient observer, because of the internal details revealed; (b) the moth, the hair; (c) her aging; the fact nobody cares about the new clothes she's bought; (d) an 'unfilial' one – the daughter will loosen her ties to her mother (almost) completely; (e) she shakes her beautiful hair to attract his attention – there is a sexual implication; (f) that her daughter will leave her, as she did her own mother.)
- Activity 4 looks at three important and, perhaps, 'difficult' phrases. (Answers: (a) they keep their secrets, and don't let them die, but look after them; (b) their was no real pattern in their life together when the girl was little – maybe a divorce? – it was all invented as they went along; (c) she openly tosses the long hair she knows is beautiful to attract the boy's attention, thus showing she's more interested in an unknown boy than her own mother.)
- Activity 5 works on irony. (Answers: (a) the mother behaves like an adolescent, while her daughter doesn't, although she is one!; (b) it's ironical that the only one who'll notice the new clothes is her sister, who will only be interested in the price, not how nice they are; (c) it's ironical that her own daughter is doing to her exactly what she did to her mother.)
- (Answer: The poem's structure is very loose – five verses (sections) of 3–6–7–4–7 lines respectively; variation of line length; no patterning of language (e.g. alliteration); one metaphor ('unreins her filly's mane' – horse's hair for girl's.)

Plenary (10 minutes): Activity 7. Students speculate. (Possible answers: they might start talking, initiated by one or the other; the girl will soon leave home and rarely visit.) Use this to start an experience-based class discussion.

Homework: Ask students to write a dialogue, started by the mother when they're home from the café, as she tries to build bridges. You might give them a start such as:

> Mother: Listen, Julie, can we just sit down for a few minutes and talk.
> Julie: Talk about what?
> Mother: About you and me.
> Julie: Well, it wasn't very nice the way we were with each other in Bewley's just now, was it?

Differentiation: You will need to be careful in dealing with these topics with students because of the high levels of broken families and different types of living arrangements.

TASK SHEET: **Mother and daughter**

1. What different ways can a mother–daughter relationship develop between the girls at the ages of 13 and 18? Think of both positive and negative scenarios and their causes. Why is this usually different from the girl's relationship with her father? Discuss your ideas in a group of four.

2. Read the poem 'Mother and Daughter in Bewley's Café'. (NB: Bewley's Café is a famous café in Dublin.)

3. Answer these questions:
    a) Who is the narrator?
    b) What physical features do they both share?
    c) What two things in verse 3 make the mother *sullen*
    d) What future do they both seem to see in verse 4?
    e) What does the girl do in relation to the boy in verse 5?
    f) What does the mother see?

4. Explain the significance of these phrases:
    a) 'they nurse their secrets'
    b) 'a makeshift past'
    c) 'frankly unreins her filly's mane'
    Check your answers with a partner.

5. Explain the irony in these phrases:
    a) 'Gazes sullen as an adolescent'
    b) 'Except her sister who'll first ask how much'
    c) 'sees what her mam saw'
    Discuss your ideas with a partner.

6. How is this poem structured?

7. What do you think is wrong in this relationship? What could they do to improve it?

Dead mother, dead wife

Introduction: In this close examination of a family, Tony Harrison explores the feelings between himself and his father, and their roots, immediately after the death of his mother.

Aims and outcomes
* To analyse a tightly structured poem
* To discuss the feelings and emotions surrounding a death

Resources required: You will need the poem 'Book Ends I', which was originally published in *Editons*; it can be found in Tony Harrison (1987) *Selected Poems*. London: Penguin Books. It is available online at:

http://plagiarist.com/poetry/5615
www.poetryconnection.net/poets/Tony_Harrison/5546

If the students enjoyed this poem, then you might want to give them the second part of the poem, which is available in the same places.

Lesson starter (10 minutes): Give out the task sheets and ask the students to do Activity 1. Once they have thought and then discussed, call back some words and ideas. You might start a word bank on the board.

Main lesson (40 minutes)
* Hand out/display the text, and ask students to read it.
* Ask them to work through the four questions in Activity 3, then discuss them with a partner. (Answers: (a) the mother/wife has died, and it was unexpected; (b) the poet, Tony Harrison himself – it is an autobiographical poem; (c) his father; (d) the poet and his father have always sat at either side of the fire, like 'bookends' on a shelf, without communicating; the irony is that the poet identifies 'books' (i.e. his learning – he is the 'scholar') as being what is between his ability to communicate with his father.)
* Activity 4 examines a detail. (Answer: they used to sit at either side of a coal fire, and could stare into the 'real' and variable flames; now there's a gas fire, with boring regular small 'buds' of flame, no good for brooding staring.)
* In this activity, students examine the formal structure and layout of the poem. The poem has six couplets, a single line, and a triplet. In fact, it's a kind of broken-up sonnet – there are 14 lines, and the rhyme scheme is ABAB; CDCD; EFEF; GHGH, in perfect rhyme. Most lines are 10 syllables long (1, 6, 9 have 9 syllables each).
* Activity 6 asks students to analyse three sets of alliteration. (Answers: (a) it thuds, like a funeral drum, or the nails being put into a coffin – heavy, dull sounds; (b) the /s/ sound is like the whisper of sleeping; (c) the 'sh' and 'sm' and 't' and 'th' sounds in *shattered* and *smithereens* really sound like something being broken, helped by the changing vowel sounds through the line.
* The students analyse the tone and emotions expressed. (Answer: it's quite a quiet poem, but it has an underlying feel of resentment and resignation, and, finally, realization about the problem, which is rather ironic, given that the title came from what his mother said about them).
* Activity 9 asks them to examine the feelings of the two men, and look for differences. (Answer: the father is plainly destroyed by the unexpected loss of his wife, and is frightened of the future. The son seems more calm about the situation, more concerned with how he might

(*continued on page 88*)

TASK SHEET: **Dead mother, dead wife**

1. How do people feel when somebody close to them dies? Think about scenes on TV or in films that you have seen where this happens. Discuss your ideas with a partner.

2. Read the poem 'Book Ends I' by Tony Harrison.

3. Decide the answers to these questions:
    a) Who has died? Was it expected?
    b) Who is the narrator?
    c) Who is the 'you' of the poem?
    d) What is the significance of the title of the poem and the problem?
    Discuss your answers with a partner.

4. What is the difference between the quoted mother's use of *grate* from the past, and the present situation as described in the fifth couplet?

5. Look at the structure of the poem and describe it in detail.

6. Explain the effect of:
    a) the /d/ alliteration in the first line
    b) the /s/ alliteration of line 6
    c) the pattern of sounds, with some /s/ alliteration, in line 13
    Discuss your ideas with a partner.

7. What is the overall feeling of this poem?

8. Do you detect any difference in feeling between the father and the son?

9. Work in a pair. Set yourselves up as described in the poem, with one the son, the other the father. Work out the kinds of attempted conversations they might have had that evening.

manage to communicate with his father with his mother there to say they are *alike*. Their focus is different.)

- Although it says in the poem 'We never could talk much, and now don't try' it would be interesting to pair the students to imagine what they might have said when they tried occasionally to talk, and how the feelings expressed in the poem might come out. Use the answers to the previous activity to help the students get into role. If they wish, they can script a dialogue, or they can just try to improvise it straight out. If you – and they – wish, have them 'perform' it for another pair or other pairs.

Plenary (10 minutes): Ask students to assess the effectiveness of the poem, and how, unlike much modern poetry, it works with very strict formal constraints – ask whether they feel that helps or hinders the meanings and effect.

Homework: Ask them to write an analysis of the poem, both its content and form (250 words).

Differentiation: You might need to tackle Activity 1 – and the poem – with care, depending on what has happened recently in the students' personal lives. On the other hand, if a student who has lost someone close recently is able to speak, it might put the whole lesson on a different dimension.

I long to see my mother

Introduction: In this lesson students relate an American short-short story to the song that inspired it, and then explore the themes of both the song and the story.

Aims and outcomes
* To relate two different types of text (song/short-short story) to each other
* To explore the themes and structure of the short-short story, which is the main focus

Resources required: The short-short story 'Mother' by Grace Paley, which can be found in Robert Shepherd/James Thomas (Eds) (1986) *Sudden Fiction: American Short-Short Stories*. London: Penguin Books; and Grace Paley (1994/2005) *The Collected Stories*. London Virago Press. It is also available online at:

 http://readashort.blogspot.com/2008/06/mother-by-grace-paley.html

You can find out about the Indiana State Song on the website.

Lesson starter (10 minutes): Give out the task sheet and ask students to read the words of the song; play the YouTube recording if you feel it is appropriate. Ask them to respond to it immediately, without looking at the questions in Activity 2.

Main lesson (35 minutes)
* Ask students to do Activity 2 individually, then check their answers with a partner. Call back ideas from the whole class. (Answers: it's about a man who is living far away from his birthplace near the Wabash River in Indiana; he feels sad, because he is remembering growing up there in the beautiful countryside, and especially he realizes how much he misses his mother, who we presume is now dead.)
* Hand out/display the Grace Paley story 'Mother' and ask students to read it. Ask for quick answers to Activity 4 from the whole class. (Answer: the writer's own thoughts of her mother are brought back by hearing the song on the radio.)
* Activity 5 asks students to purse the *doorway* theme through the story and note the related situations. You might list their answers on the board. It's important to emphasize that each doorway appearance is linked with criticism of actions, and, in two cases, worry about the writer's future. That is different from the positive memory of the mother greeting the boy in the song. (Answers: (1) front door: tells writer off for coming home late, worrying about the future; (2) writer's room door: tells writer off about political leanings; (3) kitchen door: she worries about the writer's eating, and other, habits, and future; (4) living room door: before joining her husband to listen to music.)
* Students reread the story to glean information about the parents' background. (Answers: they are immigrants, presumably from Russia [given what is said about communists]; they had to learn English when they arrived. The father is a doctor, and did well in his studies. The mother gave up her job in a shop to become a housewife, presumably once he was established as a doctor. She worries about their relationship; he's tired after work. They enjoyed listening to classical music together.)
* Activity 7 asks students to look at the structure of the story, and the significance of the repeated line 'Then she died'. (Answers: The first time it occurs after the three examples of the writer being criticized by his mother. These are all negative experiences, which are cut dead by 'Then she died'. So there is no expression of positive feelings between them, though, immediately afterwards, the author draws a set of positive other images, not related to

(continued on page 92)

TASK SHEET: I long to see my mother

1. Read the first verse and chorus of this song:

   On the Banks of the Wabash, Far Away
   Round my Indiana homestead wave the cornfields,
   In the distance loom the woodlands clear and cool.
   Oftentimes my thoughts revert to scenes of childhood,
   Where I first received my lessons, nature's school.
   But one thing there is missing in the picture,
   Without her face it seems so incomplete.
   I long to see my mother in the doorway,
   As she stood there years ago, her boy to greet.

   Chorus

   Oh, the moonlight's fair tonight along the Wabash,
   From the fields there comes the breath of newmown hay.
   Through the sycamores the candle lights are gleaming,
   On the banks of the Wabash, far away.

2. This is the State Song of Indiana, and the Wabash is the name of a river. What is the song about? What is the singer's situation? How does he feel and why? Discuss your ideas with a partner.

3. Read the American short-short story 'Mother' by Grace Paley.

4. What is the link with the song?

5. List the doorways the writer visualizes the mother in, and note what happened in each. What situation occurs each time? Check your ideas with a partner.

6. What do you find out about the writer's parents?

7. What is the significance of the repeated line 'Then she died', and its position in the story?

8. How does the writer feel about the mother? What do you think the writer thinks about her parent's relationship? What is the tone of this story? Discuss your answers with a partner.

doorways. The second part of the story relates to the mother and the father, and ends with a negative 'quarrel' in which the mother regrets them not talking any more, and the father wanting silence. This is equally cut off unresolved by 'Then she died'. The implication is that both the author and her father didn't give anything back to the mother/wife who worried about them and their relationship.)

Plenary (15 minutes): Activity 8 acts as a good way to round off work on the story. Once students have thought about the answers, you can call them back for a general discussion about what is going on in this story. (Answers: the writer regrets the mother's death, ('I have often longed . . .' maybe because she feels that there is more needed to be said by her to her mother. She paints, initially, a positive picture of the parents enjoying Mozart together – they seem as 'young' as when they first arrived in the USA. But then she remembers the unhappy scene of broken communication, also related to music. The overall tone is one of regret, even though it is not overtly stated.)

Homework: Ask students to write a dialogue between their mother (or father) and themselves, when she (he) criticized them for some action of which they did not approve. It doesn't have to be verbatim, rather they should invent what was – or would be – said. It can be completely imaginary if they wish.

Differentiation (of homework): Students from different families will have had different experience with regard to parental criticism, so allow them freedom to interpret the task as variously as suggested.

Introduction: This is an essay-writing activity in which students are asked to compare the content of a poem with that of a short-short story. If you have done lessons 4.3 and 4.4, they will be well-prepared about each text separately.

Aims and outcomes
- To compare and contrast the content of two texts
- To write an essay

Resources required: The poem 'Book Ends I' by Tony Harrison, and the short-short story 'Mother' by Grace Paley. *See* the notes to Lesson Plans 4.3 and 4.4 for the references.

Lesson starter (15 minutes – longer if they haven't done 4.3/4.4): Give students the task sheet and ask them to reread the two texts in 4.3 and 4.4. If you haven't done the previous two activities, have them read the texts and ask some of the questions on the previous two task sheets.

Main lesson (35 minutes)
- Ask students briefly to answer Activity 2 in open class. (Answers: both poems are related to the death of a mother; they both refer to the child/author, their mother, their father.)
- Ask students to do Activity 3 individually, then compare/share their ideas with a partner. Collect ideas from the whole class in a similar table on the board, as this will form the basis to their essay. (Answers: similarities: mother is dead; child/writer examines the past; child/writer feels a sense of regret; despite focussing on one parent, in both texts the other parent is referred to tellingly; both texts are autobiographical; in both texts certain features of the house [e.g. fire, armchairs, doorways] give a certain minimal setting to the content; differences: in the poem the child/writer concentrates on his difficult relationship with his father, while in the story the child/writer focuses on her relationship with her mother; in the poem, the child writer mentions his education as being the barrier, while in the story, the writer implies her mother's criticism was a barrier.)
- Again, in Activity 4, allow students to work through the texts individually to answer the questions, then compare with a partner, before collecting ideas from the whole class. (Answers: in the poem, the writer sees his dead mother as the one who held his relationship with his father together; now she's dead, there is nothing to say, as they are separated by education and *books*; in the short story, the mother is a worrier, and she presents examples of her worrying about her [the writer] and about the father/husband. In the poem, the poet feels regret more about his poor relationship with his father than about his mother's death, which his father is much more affected by; in the story, the author feels regret about not seeing her mother any more, even though she only remembers being told off.)

Plenary (10 minutes): Run through the information they have again, and discuss the suggested structure in Activity 6.

Homework: They should write the essay as homework.

Differentiation: Students can choose whether to use the suggested structure or one of their own.

TASK SHEET: **Comparing written experiences**

1. Reread the poem 'Book Ends I' by Tony Harrison, and the short-short story 'Mother' by Grace Paley.

2. What is the link in terms of the theme and the characters?

3. Think about the content. In what ways are the two pieces similar, and in what ways are they different? Make notes in the table below.

Similarities	Differences

Discuss your ideas with a partner.

4. Concentrate on the character of the mother. Decide how she is portrayed in each text. Now do the same for the father. Compare your answers with a partner.

5. What are the feelings of the 'child' (i.e. the author) towards the mother and father in each case?

6. Write a 300-word essay comparing the content of the two texts. Title: 'Compare and contrast how the two writers treat the death of their mothers'. You could use the following structure:
   Paragraph 1: introduce the two sources (c. 50 words)
   Paragraph 2: discuss the similarities (c. 100 words)
   Paragraph 3: discuss the differences (c. 100 words)
   Paragraph 4: make a conclusion (c. 50 words)

An unknown aunt

Introduction: In this lesson students read a poem about an eccentric aunt whom the writer never met, and students do some detective work to decide what it is about.

Aims and outcomes
- To read and understand a contemporary poem

Resources required: The poem 'The Aunt I Never Met' from Matthew Sweeney (1992) *Cacti*. London: Secker & Warburg (Resource Bank).

Lesson starter (15 minutes): Ask students about their aunts. Define an aunt. Invite them to say how many aunts they have, whether they are close to an aunt (or more than one), how important aunts have been in their lives.

Main lesson (35 minutes)
- Hand out the task sheets, and ask students to do Activity 1. Call back some answers, and try to elicit different reasons about why they never met these relatives. You could list the reasons on the board (e.g. lived too far away, emigrated, reclusive, ill, black sheep).
- Hand out the poem 'The Aunt I Never Met' and ask students to read it. Do Activity 3 immediately, in a whole-class setting. (Answer: *Ulster*).
- Ask students to find out the given word definitions; this could be a dictionary activity if you felt it appropriate. (Answers: (a) a sharp rectangular knife for cutting up meat; (b) a drink of vodka and tomato juice; (c) where many people meet together to play the card game 'whist'; (d) a small car with a motorcycle engine, and either a lifting top (Heinkel, Messerschmidt) or an opening front door (Isetta) – popular in the 1950s; (e) very thin crisp toast, eaten with fish or paté.)
- Activity 5 follows on with verbs. (Answers: (a) to write the number 7 in the continental European way, with a line across the upright; (b) to attract visitor.)
- Depending on their knowledge of twentieth-century history, students may not know about Eire's involvement with the Germans in World War II. (Answers: she learnt German – so as to be able to communicate with potential invaders; she wrote her 7s like a German would; she lit bonfires to help incoming German (or sympathetic) ships land with supplies of arms; and this was all bad and unsuccessful.)
- Students have to use what they have read to speculate. (Possible answers: adjectives: eccentric, outrageous, shocking, unusual, original, unconventional; presumably the author's parents regarded her as a 'black sheep' who would not be a good influence on him – also, if the knew 'she hated kids', then they knew he would not have been welcome as a child; probably he would have liked to meet such 'different' kind of person – she might have been attractive to him.)
- Students again speculate, based on what they have read. (Possible answer: she ended her life alone, so probably hating kids meant that no man would marry her.)
- Activity 9 might prove more difficult than with other poems, because there is very little in the way of structure to hang onto. (Answers: the poem has 24 lines. Their syllable length varies from 5 to 12, with 7–8–9 syllables being most frequent. Only four sentences begin at the start of a line, while five begin in the middle of the line; only four lines begin with a capital letter, the others all start with small letters, and are in the middle of sentences. Of the nine sentences, four of them begin with 'She' and the last two begin with 'Why else did . . .' It is fair to say it is a good example of free-form blank verse. There are no techniques used – everything is literal, there are no sound patterns. It is the way it is presented on the page which makes it into a poem.)

(*continued on page 98*)

TASK SHEET: **An unknown aunt**

1. Are there any members of your family who are alive whom you have never met? Or are there some family members who have died, but whom you could have met in the last ten years, but didn't? Why haven't you met them? What do you know about this person/these people? Tell a partner about one or two of them.

2. Read the poem 'The Aunt I Never Met' by Matthew Sweeney.

3. Where does this story take place? What clues helped you understand this?

4. What are these things?
   a) a cleaver
   b) a Bloody Mary
   c) a whist drive
   d) a bubblecar
   e) French toast
   Check your answers with a partner.

5. What are these actions?
   a) she . . . crossed her sevens
   b) to lure visitors

6. What is the significance of these lines?

   > *During the war*
   > *she took up German, crossed her sevens,*
   > *lit the odd bonfire at night*
   > *on the cliff edge, and did no good.*

7. What adjectives would you use to describe the aunt's behaviour? Why did this stop the author from ever meeting her? Do you think the author would have liked to meet her? Why/why not? Discuss your ideas with a partner.

8. What is the significance of these lines?

   > *She hated kids – her eventual undoing,*
   > *if you ask me.*

9. Describe the structure of the poem.

Plenary (10 minutes): Write on the board 'Is this a poem?' And ask students to discuss, then feedback to the whole class, giving reasons why or why not.

Homework: Ask them to write 100 words about either 'Why this is not a poem' or 'Why this is a poem', and to defend their title with points illustrated from the poem.

Differentiation: The opening activities give all students a chance to use their different backgrounds to get into the topic of the poem. The homework allows for them to argue a different view on what they have read.

Granny

Introduction: In this lesson, students encounter another style of writing – D. H. Lawrence's intense modernist characterisation.

Aims and outcomes
- To read, analyse and enjoy a fine piece of character and relationship description
- To plan and act out the scene

Resources required: The text of D. H. Lawrence's novella *The Virgin and the Gipsy*, Chapter 2, from 'What the girls minded most . . .' to '. . . year after year, for generations.' This is available in the cheap Wordsworth Classics edition *The Virgin and The Gipsy and Other Stories* (1990, Ware: Wordsworth Editions) or online at:

 http://ebooks.adelaide.edu.au/lawrence/dh/virgin

Lesson starter (5 minutes): Ask students to describe one (or both!) of their grandmothers to a partner, both physically, and in terms of their character.

Main lesson (40 minutes)
- Ask students to read the 'Background' to the story in Activity 1, and then make notes about their ideas in Activity 2. They can then compare these with a partner, and feed back in a whole-class setting; you may want to list their ideas about the difficulties on the board for future reference.
- Hand out the extract from *The Virgin and the Gipsy* and ask students to read it. Ask them to do Activity 4 immediately. Call back ideas from the whole class. (Answers: (a) everyone sits in the living room and Granny dominates, so no-one can be natural; (b) unhappy, aggressive, ready to be upset about everything, protective of her mother; (c) she is annoyed by her dominance, but also recognizes that she is remarkable for an old woman; (d) Granny uses Lady Louth to dominate and control situations, and because of the snob value of knowing a 'Lady' [NB the 'King Charles's Head' reference comes to Mr Dick's obsession in Dickens' *David Copperfield*])
- Activity 5 looks at the way Lawrence uses colourful language to paint his characters and their situations. Ask students to answer individually, then check with a partner. You may want to make this into a dictionary activity. (Answers: (a) refers to Granny – she's like a figure that is worshipped, who just sits there [think of a Madonna in a Roman Catholic church or a Buddha in a temple] – but the words *awful* and *old flesh* paint a very negative image; (b) *acrid* refers to an unpleasant smell, and so its use here is unusual and striking – as if Aunt Cissie emanates some kind of protective poison which keeps people away from her mother; (c) refers to the young guests, but is unusual, because *stuffed ducks* keep still, yet they are *fidgeting* – they are behaving formally, and yet are very bored; (d) Aunt Cissie is apparently very polite to her niece, but is very angry at her inside, so she is 'over-polite', and the acidity of her true feelings can be perceived; (e) the young guests [compare this simile with (c)] are not really saying anything, just going through the motions of polite conversation.)
- Activity 6 asks for close analysis of Yvette's feelings towards her Granny. She believes that Granny is actually nosey, prying into people's lives, and eating them all up like the toad she saw with the bees. She senses Granny's ability to control the situation (*something stony, relentless – her unsavoury power*). There are also lots of negative words about what Granny is like in Yvette's train of thought
- Activity 7 asks students to return to their own family and decide whether their grandmothers

(continued on page 102)

TASK SHEET: **Granny**

1. Read the background to the story extract you are going to read:

   Background to *The Virgin and the Gipsy* by D. H. Lawrence

   Cynthia Saywell left her husband, the Reverend Arthur Saywell, and daughters Lucille (9) and Yvette (7) for a younger, penniless man, causing great scandal. After this, the rector – aged 47 – moved to the tiny village of Papplewick in the north of England, and brought his almost blind mother (known as Mater and Granny), his unmarried sister (Aunt Cissie) and brother (Uncle Fred) to live with them. The girls went away to a Swiss finishing school, and returned to the village aged 21 and 19, where they found family life difficult. Lucille got a job in the city, to which she travelled daily.

2. What do you think the sisters might find 'difficult' about family life when they return home? Note three possible issues:

   1 _____

   2 _____

   3 _____

3. Read the extract from *The Virgin and the Gipsy* (from 'What the girls minded most . . .' down to '. . . for generations.').

4. Answer these questions generally from what you have read:
   a) What is the problem when Lucille and Yvette's friends visit them?
   b) What is Aunt Cissie like?
   c) What is Yvette's dual attitude to Granny?
   d) What is the significance of Lady Louth? (NB a 'King Charles's Head' means an obsession)

5. Explain the meaning of these phrases describing people's behaviour, and why they are appropriate to the people they describe:
   a) 'like some awful idol of old flesh'
   b) 'keeping an acrid guard over her'
   c) 'like stuffed ducks, fidgeting on their chairs'
   d) 'with vitriolic politeness'
   e) 'like a shoal of fishes dumbly mouthing at the surface of the water'

6. At the start of the extract, when friends comment on Granny's *interest in life* Yvette contradicts this by saying it's *an interest in people's affairs*. Relate this to what Yvette thinks in the final long paragraph and the metaphor of the toad.

7. Are either of your grandmothers like Granny? What do they do that is similar? Or is there another member of your family who is the same? Discuss your answers with a partner.

8. Act out the scene from 'Oh, come in!' to 'It was a mercy when the friends departed.' in a group of eight (Lucille, Yvette, Granny, Aunt Cissie, Lottie, Ella, Bob Framley, Leo Wetherell). Decide how to set up your acting space like the living room, what movement there will be, and who says what to whom. Remember that silence is important, too, in this scene.

(or another member of the family) control the situation, and, if so, how they do it. Ask them to discuss their conclusions with a partner, and then call back some of their experiences in a whole-class setting and see if any common pattern of control emerges.

- In Activity 8, the students need to be in groups of 8 (you can lose one or two of the guests if the numbers in your class don't add up). Give them time to work out a setting, and to plan the initial positions and movement of the scene, as well as fitting in the conversation.

Plenary (timing depends on the number of groups): Have the groups perform their take on the scene for each other, and encourage positive feedback and suggestions for improvement.

Homework: Students write a description of one of their grandmothers, in terms of both physical appearance, character and relations with others.

Differentiation: The work offers students the opportunity to explore how different people behave to each other, both in the text, and in relation to their own family; you will need to allow for the fact that some students may not have or be close to their grandmothers – these students can talk and write about other members of the family, or friends.

A grandfather

Introduction: In this lesson students read and analyse a poem which is full of metaphor and simile, a symbolic portrait of his deceased grandfather from when he was a sick child.

Aims and outcomes
- To analyse and understand a highly symbolic piece of poetry
- To write a symbolic paragraph about their own grandfather

Resources required: The poem 'In Memory of My Grandfather' from Edward Storey (1969) *North Bank Light.* London: Chatto & Windus (Resource Bank).

Lesson starter (10 minutes): Have a show of hands for living grandparents (all 4, 3, 2, 1, none?), then for preferences (grandmothers or grandfathers?). You might say something interesting about one of your grandparents and ask students for similar contributions.

Main lesson (40 minutes)
- Activity 1. Once they have made notes, encourage them to share notes and compare; suggest that their partner's notes might give them new ideas about their own grandfather.
- Activity 3. Students read and answer. (Answers: (a) he's dead now; (b) he lives in a city; (c) he must have had an extended illness (NB: *blankets* in verse 4; the whole of verse 7).)
- Students give general answers (Answer: the outside, country world of growing, living things, life itself), then specific examples (Answers: verse 1 *like an old tree* (simile)/*his voice rough as the bark of his cracked hands* (double one – simile plus metaphor); verse 4 – metaphor – *he was winter and harvest*; verse 5 – *Plums shone in his eyes* (metaphor); verse 6 – *he walked from my ceiling of farmyards* (metaphor); verse 7 – *to burst like a tree from* my *four walls* (simile).
- Activity 5. Explaining more complicated images. (Answers: (a) that he seemed to fill up the space with his 'wildness'; (b) as a child he knew what things were like because of his grandfather's descriptions; (c) he could imitate bird song, and his large beard hid his mouth; (d) he became the thing he was describing, so intense were the descriptions; (e) as a child the author visualizes the things his grandfather describes on the ceiling, then returning to his wild world from the normality of the house; (f) the child never got this close to him again – perhaps he died [*there was no chance*]?)
- Activity 6. Interpretation of information. (Answers: the author as a child loved the intensity, smell and touch of his grandfather (*I was glad of his coming. Only/through him could I breathe in the sun and smell of fields*) and the tedium of when he's not here (*The house regained silence and corners*); now he realizes how much his grandfather influenced his life and loved him.)
- (Answer: There are 8 four-line verses; no rhyme/chime; lines based around 10 syllables, varying from 7 to 11, with 8 and 9 syllable lines frequent. Each sentence starts with a capital, and all verses but three are end-stopped, so the next verse automatically starts with a capital; he does this in verse 4, too, after the semicolon, maintaining the pattern.)

Plenary (10 minutes): Ask students to call out natural images associated with the grandfather, line by line (e.g. weather – tree – bark – roots – sun – fields – soil – geese and cows – birds – singing – winter – harvest – plums – orchards – apple – core – juice – farmyards – forest of thunder – tree) so they can feel the strength of piling up these images one onto another.

Homework: Ask students to do Activity 8 for homework, writing about one of their grandfathers through a series of images that define him, having first decided what kind of person he is.

Differentiation: If students don't have a grandfather they feel they know/knew well enough to write about, it can be a grandmother or another relative instead, or even a friend or neighbour.

TASK SHEET: **A grandfather**

1. Think about your own grandfathers. Make some notes about them – for example, what they do, what you do with them, how often you see them, some good memories you have of them, what you know about them if they have already passed away.

Maternal grandfather	Paternal grandfather

Share your notes with a partner. How are you grandfathers the same and different?

2. Read the poem 'In Memory of My Grandfather' by Edward Storey.

3. Find out these things:
   a) is the grandfather alive or dead now?
   b) where is the author now?
   c) what was the author's situation at the time that he is remembering?

4. The grandfather stands as a symbol of what for the author? Find the similes and metaphors used which indicate this.

5. What do you understand by:
   a) the second sentence in verse 2?
   b) the first line of verse 4?
   c) the second and third lines of verse 4?
   d) the first sentence of verse 5?
   e) the first sentence of verse 6?
   f) the first sentence of verse 8
   Check you ideas with a partner.

6. What was the author's attitude to his grandfather's visits then? And what is his feeling about him now?

7. Analyse the structure of the poem.

8. Choose one of your grandfathers, and write a paragraph of 50–75 words about him, using suitable metaphors and similes to describe what he is like.

Introduction: This writing lesson gives students practice a writing a factual description in an organized way.

Aims and outcomes

- To write a factual description, logically ordered in paragraphs, proceeding from most important to least important information.

Resources required: A sheet of A3 paper for each student.

Lesson starter (15 minutes): Ask students to draw a family tree – do yours on the board to show them how, if they're not familiar with the concept. Suggest they do a rough one first, then draw a final draft on the piece of A3 paper you give them.

Main lesson (35 minutes)

- Give out the task sheets and ask students to do Activity 1 using their family tree to tell their partner details about the different branches of their family. Call back information from the whole class about their partners (e.g. John says: 'Peter's grandparents live in Wigan; his grandfather was a bank clerk.')
- Ask students to read the model opening half from the composition 'My Family'.
- Activity 3 asks students to analyse the structure of the writing. (Answers: Para 1: second: talks about the writer's grandparents; third: talks about the great uncle and aunt; fourth talks about Jeremy's family; para 2: first talks about Janet; second: talks about the Altrincham family, and concludes the mother's side; para 3: first: talks about father's family and where they live; second: George's family; . . . The paragraphs are linked by the branch of the family it discusses.)
- Activity 4 asks students to analyse what keeps the writing interesting, because a list of facts would make dull reading (emphasize this!). (Answer: he adds ('everyone in my family is a teacher!') as an amusing aside; he adds personal details – *She's my favourite family member; he's very funny; but I like them; which is a pity, because she's good fun.*)
- Ask students to draft their own composition, first noting and planning the content of the paragraphs – you could elicit an example of a plan using the model passage (e.g. para 1: Walsall family: Mum/Dad; Grandmother; Aunty Norah/Uncle Cyril; Jeremy & family; para 2: Rest of mother's family: Janet; the Altrincham branch; para 3: Dad's family: Uncle George & family . . .). Then they should write a first draft in class.
- Once written, ask pairs to exchange writing for peer correction. The primary concern is organization – is it planned well, does it follow on logically? Then, if while reading they notice any language errors, they can underline them. They should then talk about their partner's writing with them, and say what they thought was good and not so good.

Plenary (10 minutes): If someone has done a particularly good first draft that you've noticed, have them read it out (or you read it) for the rest of the class, as an extra model. Say why it's good.

Homework: Students write up a second draft based on their discussions with their partner, and any additional ideas they might have had.

Differentiation: Because of the wide range of family arrangements that might pertain, students should be allowed to organize their family tree in ways that are relevant to them, rather than with some pre-conceived idea of a correct format. And equally, their writing will reflect their own situation.

TASK SHEET: **Factual description: my family**

1. Work with a partner. Show them your family tree and describe the different parts of your family. Say where they live, how close you are to them, how often you see them, what they do, what they're like.

2. Read this text

My Family

I live in Walsall with my parents, Gordon and Sheila Hill. They are both teachers here in Walsall. My grandmother is a retired infants school teacher (everyone in my family is a teacher!), and she lives three miles away in Bloxwich. She's my mother's mother. My grandfather died when I was four, so she lives alone. We see her very often, though, as she comes to tea every Thursday, and to lunch every Sunday. She's my favourite family member after my parents. My great aunt and uncle also live in Bloxwich. We don't see them very often. Aunty Norah is my grandmother's sister-in-law. She's married to Uncle Cyril. I like him a lot – he's very funny. Their son Jeremy lives not far away in Pelsall with his wife Sybil and their son Matthew – he's only 5. We don't see them very often – just sometimes at Christmas or other family parties, but I like them, too. Jeremy isn't a teacher – he's an architect.

My mother's younger sister Janet lives in Weybridge in Surrey, where she is a junior school teacher. She only comes home during the school holidays, which is a pity, because she's good fun. She isn't married. There are some cousins of my grandmother's in Altrincham, but we only see them for weddings and funerals. And that's all there is of my mother's side of the family.

My father's family live in Buckinghamshire, around Newport Pagnell, and the area that is now called Milton Keynes. We are very close to my father's older brother George and his family, my Aunty Mary and cousin Elizabeth.

3. How is the writing organized? Make notes below:

Paragraph 1:

    first   *talks about the writer's parents*

    second

    third

    fourth

Paragraph 2:

    first

    second

Paragraph 3:

    first

    second

What links the content of each paragraph?

4. The writer gives basic facts about his family, but he keeps the reader's interest by adding extra information. Find examples of this.

5. Now write a first draft of the description of your family in the same way. Remember to organize your paragraphs carefully from most important to least important information. And don't forget to add some extra information to keep readers interested. Use a separate piece of paper.

6. When you have finished, exchange writing with a partner, and check the organization of the writing – can you follow it easily? If not, tell your partner. Also, if you notice any language problems (e.g. spelling mistakes, wrong tenses) put a pencil line underneath the words.

7. Now rewrite your description, taking into account anything your partner has said, and any additional things you have thought of. Use a separate piece of paper.

Section 5 Food: Making and Eating

Indian cooking

Introduction: This section examines to importance of food, not for nutrition, but because of the memories particular food invokes and the connections it makes for us.

Aims and outcomes
- To read, understand and enjoy a contemporary poem
- To examine the food culture of another ethnic group
- To write a paragraph about their own memories related to cooking and meals

Resources required: The poem 'Indian Cooking' by Moniza Alvi from (1993) *The Country at My Shoulder*. Oxford: Oxford University Press. You can find it online at:

 www.agiftformother.com/Mother_Poetry_Pack.pdf

Lesson starter (10 minutes): Ask students to talk about their food preferences, and elicit what different types of food they have tried and what they liked and didn't like.

Main lesson (40 minutes)
- Hand out the task sheet. Ask students to continue their discussions from the Lesson starter, focusing on Indian food and discuss their experiences. Call back answers from the whole class.
- Hand out/display the poem 'Indian Cooking', and ask students to read it.
- Ask them to find out (internet) or look up (dictionary) the meanings of the ingredients mentioned. (Answers: paprika (hot pepper); cayenne (hot pepper); dhania (coriander); haldi (turmeric); ghee (melted and clarified butter); keema (minced lamb curry with peas or potatoes); silver-leaf (a thin silver-coloured covering which is put on the surface of small cakes); chilli (hot pepper).)
- (Answer: the plate with the heaped powdered spices reminds her of an artist's palette heaped with powder-paints.)
- (Answer: a geographical similarity between the appearance of the food and the landscape of her father's country.)
- The structure is very simple. (Answer: There are three verses of three lines each. There is no rhyme or chime. The lines are often 10 syllables. The verses are end-stopped. Three of the verses are single sentences.)
- Moniza Alvi's father is from Pakistan. (Answer: the country is literally full of *fever* – illness; however, there is also the *fever* or excitement she feels about Pakistan, from what she has heard, having never been there.)
- (Answer: the poem describes the sensory appreciation the writer feels for her father's country, and her longing to experience the real thing.)

Plenary (10 minutes): Ask students to discuss how the poet gets so much into such a short space (Answers: the use of lists; the metaphors; the limitation, but intensity, of what she describes.)

Homework: The writing task should be used for homework. Try to encourage students to be adventurous in their use of metaphor and simile.

Differentiation: Asian students may have an advantage over others because of the familiarity of the topic; use their experiences to increase the class's understanding of the poem.

TASK SHEET: **Indian cooking**

1. Do you like Indian food? If so, what are your favourite meals? How often do you eat Indian food? If not, what don't you like about it? What sort of food do you enjoy? Tell a partner about your preferences.

2. Read the poem 'Indian Cooking' by Moniza Alvi.

3. Make a list of all the ingredients that are mentioned. Do you know what they all are? Compare your answers with a partner's.

4. What metaphor is used in the first verse?

5. What metaphor is started in verse 2 and continued in verse 4?

6. What is the significance of the word *fever* in the final line?

7. What is the poem's structure?

8. This poem is autobiographical; from what she says, what do you imagine the writer's situation was at the time that she refers to in this poem? Discuss your ideas with a partner.

9. Write a paragraph either:
   a) describing what you like about your mother's (or other relative's) cooking; or
   b) remembering a particular cooking-related incident from your childhood.
   Use some interesting metaphors and similes to describe the sight, smell, taste and feel of the food, and the sound of the cooking, as appropriate (120–150 words).

Traditional Indian cookery

Introduction: In this lesson, students will read a prose text taken from the introduction to a healthy Indian cookery book.

Aims and outcomes

* To analyse and understand the content and structure of a technical text
* To summarize the contents

Resources required: The extract from the introduction to Anjum Anand (2003) *Indian Every Day*. London: Headline (Resource Bank).

Lesson starter (10 minutes): Students describe a specific healthy lunch or dinner.

Main lesson (35 minutes)

* Students do Activity 1 in fours. Call back ideas from the whole class, and make a master 'Dos/ Donts' list on the board. Discuss the issues with the class.
* Give out the text. Ask students to explain the title through the 'message' of the text. (Answer: using spices in cooking improves health. Elicit 'the spice of life' as the source.)
* Activity 4. (Answer: it is an ancient Indian philosophy about how to live best, part of which is related to the way food helps us keep our bodies correctly balanced.)
* Activity 5. This could be a dictionary exercise. (Answers: (a) to keep at the best level of health; (b) the normal balance of our bodies; (c) leaving out certain foods on a regular basis – as many diets do; (d) the things which are added to mass-produced food to give flavour and colour, or to make them last longer; (e) people who are aware of the more subtle elements about producing and eating food; (f) the basic elements of something; (g) stop something happening, or make it better if it has happened.)
* Activity 6. (Answers: (a) it's all right to eat a little meat sometimes – once or twice a week perhaps; (b) yes, because it is difficult to digest raw vegetables; (c) untrue – Ayurveda believes that hot food is easier to digest. (d) it's not good to eat food which is out of season in the country where you live. (e) untrue – it's important to eat slowly and concentrate on the food, and in a relaxing situation, too.)
* Ask the whole class for an answer to this. (Answer: whole grains [e.g. brown rice, wholemeal flour] still have the fibre in them, which is essential for healthy digestion.)
* Activity 8. (Answers: examples: chilled pizza, microwave dinners, tinned soup; she says they are full of unhealthy extra ingredients.)
* Ask students to reread the final paragraph, then answer Activity 9. (Answers: the ingredients of Indian cooking have both preventative and curative powers; they are antibacterial and antioxidant – and so protect the body against disease and cancer.)
* (Answer: she uses *wove them into the fabric*, an image from cloth manufacture – to show their inseparable inclusion.)
* Analysis of text structure. (Answers: Para 1: the background to Ayurveda; para 2: examples of Ayurveda applied to diet; para 3: comments on the examples, everyday cooking; para 4: health benefits of cooking the Indian way.)

Plenary (15 minutes): Ask students to comment on everything they have read and give their reactions to the idea of cooking in this way. Get a class discussion going.

Homework: Ask them to do the summary of the text in 80 words – you could suggest 20 words of summary for each paragraph.

Differentiation: This topic may be familiar to some Asian – and other – students. Use their knowledge to help those to whom it is unfamiliar understand.

TASK SHEET: Traditional Indian cookery

1. What do you know about healthy eating? Get into a group of four and make a list of *dos* and *donts* for someone who wants to eat healthily.

2. Read the 'Spice Up Your Health' text.

3. What is the significance of the title of the text?

4. What do you learn about Ayurveda from the first paragraph?

5. Explain the meaning of these words and phrases:
    a) 'to maintain optimum health'
    b) 'our natural equilibrium'
    c) 'systematic deprivation'
    d) 'additives and preservatives'
    e) 'the vibration-sensitive people'
    f) 'the building blocks'
    g) 'preventative and curative powers'
   Discuss your answers with a partner.

6. Comment on the statements below in the light of Ayurvedic thinking about our diet:
    a) It's all right to eat meat regularly.
    b) You should mostly eat cooked vegetables.
    c) Cold food is easier to digest.
    d) It's wonderful that you can get frozen and imported vegetables all the year round.
    e) It doesn't matter how and where you eat as long as you eat the right kind of food.
   Discuss your answers with a partner.

7. How are *whole grains* different to *refined products*?

8. Give some examples of *convenience* meals. What does the author say about them? Compare your ideas with a partner.

9. What are the advantages of the ingredients used in Indian cooking?

10. What metaphor is used in the final sentence?

11. Look at the content of the four paragraphs of this text. How does the writer structure it?
Paragraph 1:
_____

Paragraph 2:
_____

Paragraph 3:
_____

Paragraph 4:
_____

12. Summarize the contents of the text in 80 words.

Working in a restaurant kitchen

Introduction: In this lesson, students read a piece of fiction from a contemporary novel about working in a top restaurant kitchen, but which is firmly rooted in the reality of the job.

Aims and outcomes

- Reading and understanding a prose literary extract
- Developing the vocabulary of food
- Predicting the continuation and writing it

Resources required: 2008 Orange Prize-winning novel, Rose Tremain (2007) *The Road Home*. London: Vintage (Resource Bank).

Lesson starter (5 minutes): Ask students what they know about life in a top restaurant kitchen – they have probably seen reality TV programmes with Gordon Ramsay and others.

Main lesson (45 minutes)

- Students express their own ideas about restaurant work.
- Students read the text, focussing particularly on 'foreign language' food words. This could involve dictionary/internet research. (Answers: (a) small potato or pasta 'balls' or 'dumplings' [Italian]; (b) *terrine* is a solid form of pate [French]; *mayonnaise* is a sauce made of eggs, oil, lemon juice, vinegar, salt [French]; (c) *pintade* is the French name for guniea fowl; *cèpes* is the French name for Boletus mushrooms; potatoes cooked in the oven with cheese on it [French]; (d) *halibut* is a kind of large flat fish [English]; *endives* is a kind of salad [French]; (e) literally 'burnt cream' [French] this is a kind of custard-cream dessert, where the top is burnt.) They are also asked to decide which meal they would prefer and say why – call back answers from the whole class.
- Activity 4. (Answers: (a) the gnocchi in chicken broth; (b) the *pintade*; (c) poached chicken legs with celery, carrots and gnocchi; (d) trout terrine with grapefruit mayonnaise; (e) endives.)
- Activity 5. Vocabulary work. (Answers: (a) turned quickly; (b) to put things onto clean plates; (c) French word for pastry; (d) under-chef – the second in command; (e) a herb with a purgative effect – parsley makes you urinate; (f) a French dressing made of vinegar, olive oil and herbs; (g) full of nervous energy; (h) an exciting combination of colours; (i) a sudden loud noise; (j) sharp and cleansing; (k) water-ice; (l) a 'basket' made out of sugar which has been extruded; (m) an oriental fruit; (n) a list of words with their definitions, related to a specific context.)
- Justification of ideas. (Answer: G. K. Ashe – everyone calls him 'chef'; Ashe says *I want he leaves in a rosette-shape.*; Ashe explains everything and everyone listens (e.g. *And keep it small . . . What we're saying . . . No beetroot. We discussed this.*; *Don't overcook it, then.*)
- He is mostly ignored, except when Ashe tells him things (what he has to do and that it will be difficult because of the new menu; what puddings are); they are all younger than him; they all discuss the new menu *all around him.*
- Students get into groups (G. K. Ashe, Lev, Tony, Pierre, Waldo, Sophie, Stuart, Jeb, Mario) and act out the scene, with appropriate seating and movement, and using the conversation given in the extract. They can work it out and practise in their groups, then perform it for the others.

Plenary (10 minutes): Class discussion of which performance was best and why.

Homework: Students do the writing task (Activity 9) for homework. This can be read out and/or discussed in a subsequent class.

Differentiation: Activities 7 and 8 work on the differentiation of roles in the kitchen, which can be amplified to discuss roles and status at work and in other situations.

TASK SHEET: **Working in a restaurant kitchen**

1. Based on what you know or imagine, do you think you'd like to work in a restaurant kitchen? Why/why not? Tell a partner.

2. Read the extract from Rose Tremain's novel *The Road Home* in which the Polish immigrant, Lev, starts work as a 'nurse' (i.e. doing the washing up) in the kitchen of G. K. Ashe's top restaurant.

3. Look at the meals that are mentioned:
   a) poached chicken legs with celery, carrots and *gnocchi*
   b) trout *terrine* with grapefruit *mayonnaise*
   c) *pintade* with *crèpes* and *potato gratin*
   d) *halibut* with *endives*
   e) *crème brûlée* with blueberries

   As with many menus, they contain words from other languages. Find out what the underlined words mean. Which meal would you most like to eat? Why?

4. Match the statements below with the meals in Activity 3.
   a) Lev wants to cook this for his daughter
   b) Tony wanted to use beetroot with this dish
   c) All the restaurant staff ate this for their dinner
   d) G. K. Ashe wanted to put some salad decoratively with this
   e) this will look like something from your nose if it's cooked too long

5. What do the following words and phrases mean?
   a) pirouetted
   b) replating
   c) patisserie
   d) sous-chef
   e) cleansing herb
   f) vinaigrette
   g) charged with intensity
   h) a nice vibrant colour contrast
   i) a clatter of laughter
   j) astringent
   k) sorbet
   l) a spun-sugar basket
   m) a lychee
   n) a glossary

   Check your answers with a partner.

6. Who is clearly in charge? Find some examples of things that person and other people say to show this is true.

7. What is Lev's status in this scene? Give examples which show this to be true.

8. Working in a group of nine, perform the scene, reading the dialogue, and acting out the actions described.

9. Based on what you have read in this scene, what do you think happens on Lev's first evening working at G. K. Ashe's restaurant? Write 100–150 words describing the events.

Eating avocado pears

Introduction: This lesson plan concentrates on a particular food (the avocado) through a contemporary poem about the fruit.

Aims and outcomes
* To explore a highly focussed contemporary poem
* To write a similar type of poem of their own

Resources required: The poem 'Avocados' from Esther Morgan (2001) *Beyond Calling Distance*. Tarset: Bloodaxe Books. You can also order a poster of the poem from:

 www.poetrytrust.org/learning/poetry-treatment/poem-poster-request

There are other suggestions on the website.

Lesson starter (15 minutes): Ask students to think of two very different fruits (e.g. apple/orange; strawberry/pear) and say how they are different (e.g. texture, size, shape, taste).

Main lesson (40 minutes)
* Give out the task sheet and ask students to do Activity 1. Encourage them to think about, then describe to a partner, their favourite fresh fruit, saying why they like it best. Call back some answers from the whole class – try to get them to describe size, shape, feel, texture, taste in detail.
* Distribute/Display the Esther Morgan poem 'Avocados' and ask students to read it.
* Ask them to list the five things she likes and check with a partner. Call them back and list them on the board. (Answers: (1) the size and shape; (2) the way you test if they're ripe – by squeezing the top – you might need to elicit/explain this; (3) how easy it is to cut them; (4) the feel of the 'suck' as you pull the halves apart; (5) the ease of peeling the skin off.)
* Activity 4 asks them to define the image used at the end of the first section (Answer: a metaphor: naked – like a person; a simile, likening the slippery flesh of the avocado to a wet piece of soap.)
* Activity 5 is another comprehension task. (Answers: cut into slices and covered in olive oil; cut into halves, with vinaigrette poured into the hole left by the stone.)
* Get a fuller explanation from the students. (Answer: they have a lot of calories and are fattening.)
* This activity asks students to describe the way the poet structures the content. (Answer: Section 1 talks about what avocados are like physically; Section 2 describes two ways of eating them; Section 3 gives a brief *caveat*.)
* This asks students to look at the text as a poem. (Answer: the only constant is that the first two sections are 8 lines long. There is no syllable or rhyme/chime structure. The 'shape' of the text makes it a poem.)
* Activity 9 asks students to see what the poet is doing in the poem. (Answer: the first two sections describe her pleasure in what the fruit is like, and how she likes eating it; the final two lines give an edge to this, by making the pleasure something which is almost forbidden.)

Plenary (5 minutes): Ask students what they feel about this as a piece of writing. Do they like it? Do they think it's a 'good poem'? Why/why not?

Homework: Ask them to write a similar poem in three sections, describing a fruit of their choice. Ask them to use the same structure.

Differentiation: This comes in the choice of the fruit to write about – students are free to decide their own subject.

1. Decide what you favourite fresh fruit is and why, giving details about the nature of the fruit; tell a partner.

2. Read the poem 'Avocados' by Esther Morgan.

3. What five things does the poet say she likes about avocados? Check your answer with a partner.

4. What two images does she use at the end of the first verse to describe them once the previous things have been done.

5. She describes two ways of eating them – what are they?

6. What does the author say is the problem with avocados?

7. What is the structure of the poem, in terms of the content?

8. Is there any noticeable poetic structure?

9. What effect does the final two lines have on the previous two sections?

10. Choose another fruit – preferably one you like – and write a similar poem about it.

Making rice pudding

Introduction: This lesson asks students to work out the story in the poem.

Aims and outcomes
- Students read, enjoy and work out the story contained in the poem.
- Students write a descriptive piece about a pudding they like.

Resources required: The poem 'Pudding' from Michael Laskey (1999) *The Tightrope Wedding*. Huddersfield: Smith/Doorstop Books.

Lesson starter (10 minutes): Ask students what associations they have with the word *pudding*. List their ideas on the board.

Main lesson (40 minutes)
- Ask students to focus on rice pudding through Activities 1 and 2 – call back answers for 1 from the whole class, and then build up a recipe on the board for 2.
- Distribute/display the poem and ask them to read it.
- Activity 4 asks students to unpick the characters involved in the story. (Answers: *she* in verse 1 is the wife; *he* in verse 2 is the husband; the other *she* is the man's mother; Olga is – perhaps – the man's sister, though she could easily be another close relative, such as the man's mother's sister.)
- Activity 5 looks at verse 1. (Answers: it details how the wife tried different ways to make the rice pudding closer to her husband's mother's rice pudding.) Ask students to explain what the various ingredients mentioned are (cinnamon, nutmeg, brown sugar, caster sugar).
- Activity 6 looks at the second verse, which brings in the character of the husband. (Answers: it shows the fact that, despite all her best efforts, and despite making a lovely-sounding rice pudding, the husband is still dissatisfied because it isn't like his mother's.)
- Verse 3 provides the denouement of the plot. (Answer: that the mother used tinned Ambrosia Creamed Rice in her rice pudding – she 'cheated' – the mystery ingredient the husband craved and the wife had searched for was not natural.)
- (Answer: you *admit* to a crime – the mother was guilty of 'not playing fair'.)
- (Answer: the traditional difficult wife/mother-in-law relationship got easier once they had shared their sadness at Olga's death – they were able to talk about things they hadn't talked about before.)
- (Answer: the wife never made rice pudding again, or even a cooked pudding, just giving her husband fresh fruit for dessert. A kind of punishment.)
- In Activity 11 students analyse the structure of the poem. (Answer: three six-line verses; no rhyme or chime; line length is between 7 and 10 syllables with 8/9 most frequent.)

Plenary (10 minutes): Asks students to comment on how subtly and effectively the poet tells us a lot about the people through this one part of their lives.

Homework: Ask students to do the writing in Activity 12 for their homework. Impress on them the need for detail.

Differentiation: This is allowed for in their responses to the first two Activities. You can make the homework writing about any food if you find there are students who really don't like puddings of any kind, but keep off fruit if you have done the previous activity on avocados.

TASK SHEET: **Making rice pudding**

1. Do you like rice pudding? If so, when was the last time you ate it? What do you like about it? If not, why don't you like it? And what do you like instead? If you eat rice pudding at home, who makes it, and how often? Discuss your answers in a group of four.

2. How do you make rice pudding? What are the qualities of a good rice pudding? Work out a recipe with a partner.

3. Read the poem 'Pudding' by Michael Laskey.

4. Identify the characters. Who is the *she* of the first verse? Who is the *he* of the second verse? Who is the *her/she* who is asked and explains in the final verse. Who do you think Olga was? Check your ideas by discussing in a group of four.

Do all the next five Activities with a partner:
5. What actions does the first verse tell us about?

6. What is described in the second verse?

7. What is the discovery that is made in verse 3?

8. What is the significance of the verb *admitted* in verse 3?

9. What do you understand about the relationship between the *she* of verse 2, and the *her/she* of verse 3 before and after the death of Olga?

10. What was the result of the revelation? Why?

11. Analyse the structure of the poem.

12. Write in detail about a pudding you like. Explain who makes/buys it for you. Where and when do you eat it? What do you particularly like about it? Does it have any particular associations for you with a person, a place or something else?

Eating sushi at home

Introduction: This lesson invites the students to analyse a poem which, although apparently about eating sushi, is actually a love poem in disguise.

Aims and outcomes
- Students read and analyse a contemporary poem
- Students use the style to write a piece about a similar real or imagined event

Resources required: You will need the poem 'Sushi' from Tobias Hill (1998) *Zoo*. Oxford: Oxford University Press (Resource Bank). There is suggested sushi information on the website.

Lesson starter (10 minutes): Ask students what they know about Japan – elicit information. If they talk about Japanese food, steer the class in that direction and elicit *sushi*; otherwise introduce it yourself.

Main lesson (40 minutes)
- Students move from the class discussion to do Activity 1 in pairs. Elicit and note details on the board. (Basic information: it is a Japanese speciality consisting of boiled rice, packed into small blocks, with different types of raw/cooked fish on it; there are also cylindrical blocks of rice, wrapped in *nori* [seaweed] and with fish or vegetables in the centre; it is eaten with sliced ginger, wasabi [horseradish] paste and soya sauce)
- Students read the poem and do Activity 3. (Answers: two people [sexes not given] are eating sushi in a flat/house, in the early hours of the morning; the writer is very excited, and is obviously in love with the other person.)
- Elicit the foods mentioned, and elicit/explain what they are. (Answers: *abalone* and *ark shell* are kinds of shellfish; *bluefin* is a type of tuna fish; *red salmon eggs* – they are *tender*; *white rice*.)
- Examining the underlying meaning. (Answer: it is really a love poem, in which the writer and his partner are at a key point in their relationship – perhaps it is just going to become more intimate – and he wants to savour the moment so he can always recall it.)
- The formal structure is very loose. (Answer: eight verses of varying length (3–5 lines); lines of varying length (3–11 syllables, with 4–5–6 syllables being most frequent); no rhyme or chime; sentences within and across verses show enjambment.)
- (Answer: informal, simple; no complex words, structures or ideas; quite factual descriptions of actions and thoughts; flows naturally, like everyday speech.)
- Examination of the poet's language. (Answers: (a) regular use of alliterating /s/ sound words, indicating softness, quietness; *sweet* and *sweat* chime, *smell* and *shell* rhyme; (b) a child might scratch the chocolate off (e.g.) a chocolate biscuit to eat it separately; (c) salmon eggs are round and shiny like pearls; (d) he gets a sense of movement by repeating 'skipping along', which has a rhythmic pattern like 'skipping'; (e) repetition of the happy word *skipping*; (f) he compares how memory returns, getting nearer, bouncing safely on the water, to 'skipping (skimming) stones' – an unusual, striking image for the way memory comes back.)

Plenary (10 minutes): Ask students to say what they like/don't like about this poem, and why.

Homework: Help students with the writing task by going through the structure of the poem – the sense of time and place, the details of the food, the personal feelings, and ask students to structure their writing in a similar way, paying attention to each element.

Differentiation (of homework task): In the writing, students can use real or imagined events, from two possible starting points.

TASK SHEET: Eating sushi at home

1. Do you know what sushi is? You can buy it in Tesco, Marks & Spencer and other supermarkets now, as well as in sushi restaurants. What does it look like? What is it made of? Have you ever eaten it? If so, say what it's like. If not, do you think you'd like to try it? Why/why not? Talk to a partner about what you know.

2. Read the poem 'Sushi' by Tobias Hill.

3. Describe the situation in your own words. What are the people doing, where, when, how do they feel? Check your answers with a partner.

4. What examples of sushi foods are mentioned? How are they described?

5. Despite its title, what is this poem really about? Give reasons for your answer?

6. Analyse the structure of the poem, and describe it.

7. How would you describe the language the poet uses in this poem?

8. Examine the following parts of the poem and write a comment on each of them:
    a) Describe the patterning of sounds and words in verse 2
    b) Explain the simile in verse 3
    c) Explain the metaphor in verse 4
    d) The patterning of language and its effect in verse 6
    e) The relationship of verse 6 to verse 8
    f) The effect of the simile in verse 8
    Discuss your answers with a partner.

9. Write a paragraph (about 100–120 words) about eating something with a friend or relative, exploring what it was like (think about all the five senses), and how you and the other person felt. If you don't have an actual memory of a particular occasion, invent one (e.g. 'Eating fish and chips in the street with Michael' or 'An ice-cream on the beach with Susie').

Moules à la Marinière

Introduction: This lesson comprises a thorough examination of the language, structure and content of the poem.

Aims and outcomes

* To make a close study of the language, structure and content of a contemporary poem.

Resources required: The poem 'Moules à la Marinière' from Elizabeth Garrett (1991) *The Rule of Three*. Newcastle-upon-Tyne: Bloodaxe Books; also in Hulse M *et al.* (1993) *The New Poetry*. Newcastle-upon-Tyne: Bloodaxe Books. You can find it online at:

 www.bbc.co.uk/radio3/wordsandmusic/pip/mne6u

Lesson starter (5 minutes): Write 'Moules à la Marinière' on the board. Elicit what language it is and the meaning (mussels in the mariner's style). Show a picture.

Main lesson (45 minutes)

* Make Activity 1 brief and elicit answers quickly. (Answer: oval shape, tapering to a point at one end; blue back.) Elicit any experiences quickly, too.
* Ask them to read the recipe and comment. (Answer: they should say it's quite simple because it doesn't have lots of different ingredients or need any special preparation.)
* Distribute/display the poem 'Moules à la Marinière' by Elizabeth Garrett and ask students to read it. The language is quite complex, so give them time.
* Activity 5. (Answers: (a) in the rocks of a creek, under seaweed; (b) in a bucket behind the kitchen door; (c) it washed away the salty sea-smell.)
* For Activity 6, students will almost certainly need a dictionary to work on the 'difficult' vocabulary of the poem. (Answers: (a) the seaweed has air-sacs like 'blisters' on its leaves; (b) desired groups; (c) nursery; (d) to erase; (e) a white wine; (f) suggests; (g) longing for; (h) leaning rudely; (i) greasy blessing; (j) long robe worn by a priest; (k) sea-food (shellfish/squid/octopus); (l) the pain which comes after something hits you.)
* The poem has a high degree of formal structure. (Answer: there are four six-line verses, with a (mostly) ABBACC rhyme/chime-scheme – verse A is more difficult to define, as lines 1–2–3–6 all chime, with 2–6 an almost perfect rhyme; the lines are almost all 10-syllables long.)
* Activity 8. (Answers: (a) verse 1 [almost] w*rack/tracks*; verse 2 *recall/all*; verse 4 *away/lay; lingers/fingers*; (b) e.g. verse 1 *prised/bruised*; verse 3 *song/tongues*; (c) e.g. the /k/ sound in *kitchen clefts and clings; lewdly lolling*; (d) *yearning wide as if in song*; (e) *lewdly-lolling parrots tongues*; (f) the 'uck' and 'u' sounds *the tuck* and *chuckle of mussels in a bucket.*)
* This requires an understanding of how the poet works through her feelings about collecting, cooking and eating the mussels. (Answers: verse 1 – seems like they are stealing babies from a nursery – and the sea erases their tracks; verse 2 talks about the cooking, especially the noise the oyster shells make in the bucket, and the noise of cooking; verse 3 seems like a religious rite – napkins are cassocks, they bow their heads to eat; verse 4 is full of guilt, the desire to rid themselves of the memory of this 'crime' (the violence of 'wrenched', the 'forbidden fruit').)

Plenary (10 minutes): Discuss the poet's feelings about this meal with the whole class.

Homework: Students analyse the poem's language, structure and content in 250 words.

Differentiation: Take into account students' different experiences of and reactions to food.

TASK SHEET: **Moules à la Marinière**

1. Have you ever seen mussels at the seaside or in a fresh-fish shop? Describe their shape and colour. If you've seen them wild, where do you find them and what do they look like? Talk about this to a partner.

2. Have you ever eaten mussels? When and where? How were they served? Did you enjoy them? Why/why not? Tell a partner.

3. Read this recipe for Moules à la Marinière:

    Ingredients:
    500 ml light, dry, white wine   ½ cup if chopped shallots
    8 sprigs of parsley   ½ bay leaf
    ¼ teaspoon of thyme   ⅛ teaspoon black pepper
    100 g butter   ½ cup roughly chopped parsley
    3–4 litres scrubbed, washed mussels

    Procedure:
    Put all the ingredients except the ½ cup of parsley and the mussels into 6–8 litre covered pot and cook slowly for 2–3 minutes. Add the mussels and boil fast for 5 minutes or so, until all the mussels are open; toss the mussels in the covered pot several times as they boil to ensure they are all cooked evenly. Serve in large bowls, with some of the juice and sprinkled with the chopped parsley. You can eat them like this, or add a squeeze of lemon juice, or some cream, depending on your preference.

    Do you think it sounds like a difficult recipe? Why/why not?

4. Read the poem 'Moules à la Marinière' by Elizabeth Garrett.

5. Answer these questions quickly and briefly:
    a) Where did she get the mussels?
    b) Where did she keep them at first?
    c) What did the rain do?
    Discuss your answers with a partner.

6. Find the meaning of these words and phrases:
    a) blistered fronds   g) yearning
    b) concupiscent clusters   h) lewdly lolling
    c) crêche   i) unctuous benediction
    d) expunged   j) cassocks
    e) Muscadet   k) fruits de mer
    f) insinuates   l) after-sting
    Check your answers with a partner.

7. Analyse the formal structure of the poem, and describe it to a partner.

8. Find examples of: (a) rhyme (d) simile (b) half-rhyme/chime (e) metaphor (c) alliteration (f) assonance

9. Describe the structure of the poem, in terms of what the content is, and how it is organized; discuss your ideas with a partner.

Home-made jam

Introduction: This lesson deals with an adult reflecting on her childhood experience of her mother making jam.

Aims and outcomes
- Close reading of a contemporary poem
- Writing instructions for making jam

Resources required: The poem 'Crab Apple Jelly' from Vicki Feaver (1994) *The Handless Maid*. London: Jonathan Cape. You can find it online at:

 http://sirlancsallot.blogspot.com/2006/09/crab-apple-jelly.htm

For a recipe *see* the website.

Lesson starter (10 minutes): Ask students what their favourite jam is and what they like eating it with (e.g. bread, toast, with or without butter). Ask if there are there any jams they don't like and why.

Main lesson (40 minutes)
- Move into Activity 1 by handing out the task sheets. After they have discussed, elicit ideas from each group and compile a master recipe on the board.
- Students read the poem, then in fours list the stages of production in order. (Answers: (1) collecting wild crab apples; (2) smashing the apples against the side of the pan and cooking them; (3) straining the pulp in muslin for several days; (4) boiling the juice with sugar; (5) testing readiness by dribbling syrup onto a cold plate; (6) filling heated jars; (7) checking the jelly had cleared.)
- Activity 4 asks for closer analysis of the poem's characters and situation. (Answers: she is addressing her mother; the grandmother is mentioned; it seems as if there were problems in 'that house of women' [daughter (author), mother, grandmother].)
- Activity 5. Focusses on feelings. (Answers: she hated the pulp in the straining bag – the colour, the shape [like a head], the *sourness* – which she relates to the relationship problems; she loved and wondered at the beauty of the colour of the finished jam.)
- Activity 6 analyses the formal structure of the poem, which is rather limited. (Answers: It has seven five-line verses; there is no rhyme/chime scheme, though some line-end words do have vaguely related patterns (verse 1 *jars/sugar*; verse 2 *cherries/gooseberries*; verse 3 *pan/Wigan*; verse 4 *string/dripping*; verse 6 *sugar/jars*; verse 7 *cleared/fire*); line length varies from 5–12 syllables, with 7–8–9 being the most frequent; there is in-verse and across-verse enjambement. The phrase *every year* patterns verses 1 and 2 together.)
- This activity asks students to look at the style of language used (Answers: mostly – except for the instances noted in Activities 4 and 5 – it is very matter of fact – a simple factual description of her mother's process of making the jam, including her initial annual antagonism to it.)

Plenary (10 minutes): Students discuss what they liked/didn't like about the poem, and why.

Homework: Ask students to do Activity 8 for homework, writing an 'official' recipe (suggest they borrow one of their parents' cookery books for a model, if they're not sure about the form) for making crab apple jelly, using the details obtained from the poem.

Differentiation: Any students who would prefer it, can write a recipe of their own choice, but emphasize that it must not be copied from a book, but one they already know. They must write it formally, including ingredients and utensils.

TASK SHEET: **Home-made jam**

1. Do you know how jam is made? Does anyone in your family, or anyone else you know make their own jam? Get into a group of four and discuss what you know.

2. Read the poem 'Crab Apple Jelly' by Vicki Feaver.

3. Work in your group of four and make a list of the stages mentioned in the making of the jam. Based on your answers to Activity 1, do you think any stages are missing in the poem? Or did you miss out any stages? If so, which? What equipment is mentioned?

4. Who is the *you* who the writer addresses in the poem? Who else is mentioned? What family situation is referred to?

5. What didn't the writer like about the jam-making process and why? How would you describe her reaction to the finished jam in the final two lines?

6. Describe the formal structure of the poem.

7. How would you describe the overall style of the poem's language and presentation? What parts differ from this? Discuss your ideas in your group of four.

8. Write a recipe for a recipe book on how to make crab apple jelly, including a list of ingredients, utensils and the process.

Making a salad

Introduction: This lesson uses a nineteenth-century poem by Sydney Smith (1771–1845) to open up a discussion on salad and salad dressing.

Aims and outcomes
- To read an understand a nineteenth-century poem, complete with an older style of English
- To examine the way a traditional rhyming poem works
- To discuss salads and salad dressings

Resources required: The poem 'Recipe for a Salad' by Sydney Smith, which can be found online at this address:

 http://rpo.library.utoronto.ca/poem/2746.html

Lesson starter (5 minutes): Students discuss their different feelings about salads.

Main lesson (45 minutes)
- Activity 1. Elicit and write on the board a list of basic UK salad foods (e.g. lettuce, tomatoes, cucumber, spring onion, radishes, raw carrot, watercress, mustard and cress) but also more 'exotic' possibilities (e.g. avocado, fennel, beetroot, maize [corn], olives, Jerusalem artichokes, Spanish onion, different kinds of lettuce).
- Ask them to do Activity 2 and call back suggestions. Expect: salad cream, mayonnaise, vinaigrette, olive oil, vinegar, Thousand Island dressing, etc.
- Activity 4. Students read and discuss the poem. Elicit suggestions (Part 1 describes the process of preparing the salad dressing; Part 2 describes its effect on people.)
- Activity 5. (Answers: (1) the pounded yolks of two hard-boiled eggs; (2) two sieved boiled potatoes; (3) chopped onion; (4) a spoonful of mustard; (5) two spoonfuls of salt; (6) four spoonfuls of olive oil; (7) two spoonfuls of vinegar; (8) a soupçon of anchovy sauce.)
- Activity 6. (Answers: (a) they have to be beaten; (b) they have to boiled then passed through a sieve; (c) Lucca, in northern Tuscany, Italy; (d) small salty fishes; (e) because it *bites – mordere* is the Latin root; (f) because the onions should be chopped into tiny pieces.)
- Activity 7 looks at the equipment mentioned: a kitchen sieve, a bowl and a spoon.
- Activity 8 asks students for their opinions on the taste of the dressing. Elicit and expect a wide range of opinions, depending on ethnic and social background.
- Activity 9. This could be a dictionary activity, to find *anchorite* (hermit, recluse) and *epicure* (gourmet) and unpick the meaning. Basically, at opposite ends of the scale, the hermit who eats nothing, and the epicure with a sophisticated palate, would both be satisfied by a salad with this dressing on it.

Plenary (10 minutes): Once students have understood the poem, ask them as a whole class to describe the structure of the poem. (A 20-line poem, with rhyming couplets, each with a 10-foot line.) There are a few other elements to note, e.g. *mordant mustard* (biting alliteration!), *smoothness and softness* (the 's' consonance sounds what it intends), *green and glorious* (a notable /g/ sound).

Homework: Students can write the recipe out in a conventional prose way, listing the ingredients first, then giving the process. Ask them to look in a cookery book or on the Internet if they're unfamiliar with the style.

Differentiation: There is plenty of room to bring out different eating habits based on ethnicity and social cultural background, and to bring home the idea that 'just because it doesn't sound nice to you doesn't mean it isn't good to others' – inclusiveness.

TASK SHEET: **Making a salad**

1. What ingredients can you put into a fresh salad? Work with a partner and make a list below.

2. When you have put the ingredients together in a bowl, what can you put onto the salad to give it additional flavour? List some possibilities here:

3. Read the poem 'Recipe for a Salad' by Sydney Smith (1771–1845).

4. If I say that the poem has two parts, one lines 1–14 and the other lines 15–20, what would you say the reason for my division was? Check your ideas in a group of four.

5. Make a list of the eight ingredients the poet suggests for this *condiment* (salad dressing), with the quantity needed:

   1 _____   5 _____
   2 _____   6 _____
   3 _____   7 _____
   4 _____   8 _____

6. Work with a partner and answer these questions about the ingredients:
   a) What do you have to do to the egg yolks? _____

   b) What do you have to do to the potatoes? _____

   c) Where does the olive oil come from? _____
   d) What are anchovies? _____
   e) Why is mustard *mordant*? _____
   f) What is the intent of *onion atoms*? _____

7. What three kitchen implements and vessels are mentioned?
   1 _____
   2 _____
   3 _____

8. What do you think this salad dressing would be like to taste? Do you think you would like it? Why/why not? Discuss your ideas with a partner.

9. Look at the second part of the poem (lines 15–20). What is the poet's purpose here? Who are the two key people referred to? Write a definition.
   a) an anchorite
   b) an epicure
   What is the significance of using these two, and describing their reactions to such a dressed salad?

10. Look at the structure of the poem, and describe this.

11. Can you find any examples of alliteration, assonance, consonance or any figures of speech? If so, what is their effect?

What are scampi?

Introduction: In this lesson students compare the details of an incident from a poem with a piece of factual information.

Aims and outcomes
- Reading and analysing a contemporary poem
- Comparing the contents of the poem with a piece of factual information

Resources required: The poem 'Scampi' from Neil Rollinson (1996) *A Spillage of Mercury*. London: Cape Poetry, which can be found online at:

 www.universalmetropplis.com/city/threads.php?threadid=3857

The article 'What Is/Are Scampo/Scampi?' which is online at:

 www.ochef.com/881.htm

There are additional suggestions on the website.

Lesson starter (10 minutes): Ask the students what they know about seafood. Start with mussels if you did lesson 5.6; elicit/give the names of some common elements of the seafood category: *octopus, squid, shrimp, prawn, langoustine, crab, lobster, winkle, whelk, cockle, clam, oyster*. List them on the board. If someone offers *scampi*, write it up, but don't offer information about it, even if asked what it is.

Main lesson (40 minutes)
- Give out the task sheets and ask students to get into pairs to do Activity 1. Elicit responses from the whole class, and list ideas on the board. Even now, don't comment on what students say, just note all the ideas that come in and stimulate thinking by asking questions such as *Do you agree? What do you think? Is that correct?*
- Distribute/display the poem 'Scampi' by Neil Rollinson and ask students to read it.
- Ask students to do Activity 3 quickly, and check their answers quickly with a partner. Give them a time limit, maybe. Elicit answers from the whole class. (Answers: (a) In a restaurant; (b) his girlfriend; (c) what exactly scampi is; (d) *a cross between chicken and fish*; (e) he imagines all sorts of other unlikely crosses between animals; (f) his girlfriend, because he's playing with his food; (g) *Dublin Bay Prawns*.)
- Let the students do Activities 4, 5 and 6 individually, then discuss their ideas with a partner, before you elicit answers to the three activities, as they are all related to the nature of the poem as a poem. Activity 4: the poem has no overt repeating formal structure. (Answer: it is a continuous poem of 38 lines, broken into four sections; there is no rhyme/chime; line length varies of 3–12 syllables, with 8 and 10 syllables being most frequent.)
- Activity 5 (Answer: the poem is basically descriptive of the events in the restaurant, in simple everyday English, and with the writer's imaginative ideas – which are also in everyday spoken English – put in between those activities.)
- Activity 6 (Answer: there are 4 sections to the poem. Section 1 deals with the initial question and answer; Section 2 deals with the writer's imagined animal crosses after the waitress has gone; Section 3 deals with more outlandish imaginings until the food comes, and after; Section 4 deals with the situation in the restaurant again, and the resolution to the question.)
- Activity 7 asks for an analysis of the writers imagined crosses. (Answers: (1) chickens mating

(continued on page 130)

TASK SHEET: **What are scampi?**

1. Do you know what scampi are? Have you ever eaten them, or seen people eating them? How are they served? What do they look like? Talk to a partner.

2. Read the poem 'Scampi' by Neil Rollinson.

3. Answer these questions quickly:
   a) Where does the action take place?
   b) Who is the writer there with?
   c) What does the writer want to know?
   d) What does the waitress answer?
   e) What does the writer do for most of the poem?
   f) Who gets angry and why?
   g) What answer does the writer get to his question?
   Compare your answers with a partner.

4. Analyse the formal structure of the poem.

5. How would you describe the language used in the poem?

6. Analyse the way the content is broken down, and how this is reflected in the way the poem is laid out.

7. Discuss your answers to Activities 4, 5 and 6 with a partner.

8. List the other food crosses the writer imagines.

9. Read the article 'What Is/Are Scampo/Scampi?' at this website: www.ochef.com/881.htm

10. What in the article:
    a) Reflects the reasonableness of the writer's question and the waitress's answer?
    b) Reflects the girlfriend's answer?

11. Answer these questions about the article, with an explanation.
    a) Is the author from Britain?
    b) Is the author interested in the biology of sea creatures?
    c) Which are the best scampi and why?
    d) Where can you eat real scampi?
    Check your answers with your partner.

with fish; (2) turkeys with pterodactyl genes; (3) sheep with dolphins.)

- In Activity 9 either distribute copies of or display the article 'What Is/Are Scampo/Scampi?' and ask students to read it.
- They should then do Activity 10 quickly and individually; elicit answers quickly, too. (Answers: the author says that 'What Is/Are Scampo/Scampi? is one of the most complex questions in all of food-dom'; he later says that 'Dublin Bay Prawns' is one of the synonyms for the creatures that are known as scampi in Italian.)
- Activity 11 asks for close reading of the article. (Answers: (a) No, because he mentions 'in Britain' and also says 'at least in this country' implying he is not in Britain, and later he says 'what you get as scampi in this country' – he also uses US spelling for the word *flavor*; (b) No, because he says 'outside the world of marine biology', and it's too much trouble *at least to us* (who are not biologists); (c) the Adriatic ones, because they are meatier, have fatter tails and more flavour; (d) In the Mediterranean and Adriatic area, Morocco, Britain, possibly Norway.)

Plenary (10 minutes): Ask students to discuss what they think of the poem.

Homework: Ask students to draw one of the three animal crosses which the writer imagines.

Differentiation: Accept that many students may have no experience of scampi, and that this will actually be part of the educational point of the lesson for them. For many/most students the information in the article will be completely new.

What I'd serve

Introduction: In this lesson, students use their imagination to produce a feast for a special occasion.

Aims and outcomes
- To write a description of a special meal of their invention

Resources required: None.

Lesson starter (15 minutes): Ask students to discuss the kinds of special occasions when special food is served, and how that food is different from normal food.

Main lesson (35 minutes)
- Hand out the task sheet to the students, and explain that they are going to plan a special meal for a particular event, and write a description of it. Direct them to Activity 1 and ask them to decide on the details individually. (You may wish for some/all students to work together in pairs, which would also be a good way of doing this lesson.)
- With that done, Activity 2 asks students to decide on the issue of choice – you could have a discussion with them about the pros and cons of having a choice of foods (e.g. it's more complicated to have a choice, but more people are likely to be satisfied; you can have a meat/fish/vegetarian option; or choose something non-meaty which is acceptable to everyone.)
- In Activity 3 students move on to note down the actual food that they want to serve.
- Activity 4 gives them a template to use for the structure of their written description.

Plenary (10 minutes): Look at the language in Activity 5, which shows them the examples of conditional phrases that they can use to structure their writing.

Homework (additional 30 minutes in subsequent lesson): Ask them to write a first draft of the description for homework.
- They should bring it in next lesson for peer correction with a partner. Students should check the organization and content, and make suggestions for improvements; if they notice any language errors (e.g. spelling mistakes, wrong tenses) they should underline them for their partner to correct themselves.
- They should then produce a second draft, using their partner's suggestions and further ideas of their own, which should be handed in for you to read.

Differentiation: This activity offers students the freedom to choose what foods they would like to have.

TASK SHEET: **What I'd serve**

1. Decide on a special occasion – it can be a real one, such as your birthday, or an invented one. You are going to organize a special sit-down three-course meal for the people who attend. You do not have to worry about the cost. Decide and note the following:
    a) What is the occasion? _____
    b) Who are you going to invite? _____

    c) Where will it take place? _____
    d) When will it take place? _____
    e) What will people wear? _____

2. Think about the meal itself. Will it be a set meal, with the same food for everyone, or will there be a choice for each course?

3. Now think about the actual food you want to provide and make notes:
    a) First course: _____
    _____

    b) Second course: _____
    _____

    c) Dessert: _____
    _____

4. Now plan your written description of the event. Use this structure:
    • Paragraph 1: A short introduction (information from Activity 1 above)
    • Paragraph 2: The food for the first course, and any drinks to be served with it
    • Paragraph 3: The food for the main course, and any drinks to be served with it
    • Paragraph 4: The food for dessert, and any drinks to be served with it
    • Paragraph 5: Conclusion

5. Use conditional language to structure your event: *If I was going to . . . I would . . . the first course would be . . . I'd invite . . . We'd hold it in . . . After the dessert we'd . . . Then they would . . . Finally we'd . . .*

Section 6   On the Road

6.1 Walking to the Danube

Introduction: This lesson uses the start of a short story about a dissatisfied young city boy walking across the Romanian countryside to the Danube; if you don't know it's from a short story, it also reads like a piece of travel writing.

Aims and outcomes
- Students read, enjoy and analyse the text
- They write a similar piece of their own

Resources required: The start of the short story 'Walking to the Danube' from Philip Ó Ceallaigh (2006) *Notes from a Turkish Whorehouse*. Dublin: Penguin Ireland (Resource Bank).

Lesson starter (10 minutes): Ask the students what they know about the River Danube (e.g. start, cities/countries it flows through, end); whether anyone has seen it; how long it is (2860 km); why it's important (transport, irrigation, border), and so on. *See* the website for other information.

 http://en.wikipedia.org/wiki/Danube

Main lesson (40 minutes)
- Activity 1. When you call back experiences from the groups, try to elicit the feelings they had during and after their walk.
- Hand out/display the text, but do not say it's from a short story; students answer Activity 3 in a whole-class setting (Answer: it's the opening of a contemporary short story, though it reads like a piece of travel writing.)
- Ask students if they can answer Activity 4, too. Depending on what you did in the Lesson starter, you might like to elicit what the options are (Germany, Austria, Slovakia, Hungary, Croatia, Serbia, Romania, Bulgaria, Ukraine, Moldova). (Answer: Romania.)
- Activity 5 asks student to analyse the content, which is important for the later writing activity. (Possible answers: he uses *poetic description* 'hard shafts between breaks in bruised clouds'; the passage where he is taken around the village by the grandchildren, 'Adults learn to be ashamed', etc. – he is philosophical about life; attention to small details 'She pointed at the stream and told me she was afraid because once she had seen a snake in the water', which is unnecessary for the narrative, but gives colour and reality; expansion of some details which could have remained small – the passage about the girls' father, the marriage etc. These are all things which give 'humanity', complexity and character to the story of the journey.)
- Activity 6. Looks at how the author shows things rather than tells them – a crucial element in story-writing. (Answers: (a) She is very generous, trusting, and caring; (b) it is beautiful, though rather depressed; (c) it is bad because of the closure of factories, and people leaving.)
- Activity 7 looks at the way the content is organized. (Answer: the first part is his arrival at the village; the second part is his time with the family there; the third part is his leaving and travelling again)

Plenary (10 minutes): Ask students whether this kind of solo walk in the country is something they would like to do, and why/why not.

Homework: Ask students to write their own piece about a journey, as directed in Activity 8. Turn this into a peer-review activity, by having them exchange writing and redraft in the next lesson.

Differentiation: The options in the homework allow students to draw on real or imagined journeys; the peer-review activity allows them to share their writing with others and redraft, rather than hand it in to you for arbitration.

TASK SHEET: **Walking to the Danube**

1. What was the longest walk you have ever done? Where, when and why did you do it? Who did you did it with? What did you feel while you were doing it and after? Did you enjoy it? Why/why not? Get into a group of four and share your experiences.

2. Read the extract from 'Walking to the Danube' by Philip Ó Ceallaigh.

3. What kind of text is this? Where do you think it came from? What is its purpose?

4. From the names of the people and places, which Danube country do you think this takes place in?

5. 'This text does not just give facts about what the writer did on his walk.' Find some examples which show this statement to be true.

6. Describe what these things are like:
    a) The old lady in the village of Ilidia
    b) The countryside
    c) The economic situation in the area
    Check your answers in your group of four.

7. The content of this text has three different parts. What would you say they are?

8. Write a description of a journey that you made, which has three similar parts to this one. Try to include some specific details about things, as this text does. You can invent a journey, if you don't want to use a real one (250–300 words).

9. When you have finished the first draft of your writing, exchange it with a partner. Read their work, and comment on it in terms of:
    a) Whether it was easy to follow
    b) If you feel the language or the organization could have been better, explain what changes you would make. When you have discussed each other's work, rewrite it in the light of the comments made, if you feel they were valid.

Hard travelling

Introduction: This lesson looks at the text of a famous song written by the American singer Woody Guthrie in 1959, examining the narrator's situation.

Aims and outcomes
- To listen to, understand and enjoy a famous song from another culture
- To relate the content to a British folk song

Resources required: The lyrics of Woody Guthrie's song 'Hard Travelin'', which can be found online at:

 www.woodyguthrie.org/Lyrics/Hard_Travelin.htm

This is the official Woody Guthrie website, where much information can be found about him. For other suggestions *see* the website.

Lesson starter (10 minutes): Ask students what reasons people have had for leaving home and moving around in past centuries – list their suggestions. If you don't get 'looking for work' as an answer, elicit it.

Main lesson (35 minutes)
- Give students the task sheet, and ask them to do Activity 1 with a partner. Elicit answers from the whole class. (Possible answers: a lot of travelling around, living in bad conditions, looking for work, which was tiring and poorly paid; sleeping rough; little food; dangerous; lonely; unhealthy.)
- Give out/display the text of Woody Guthrie's song 'Hard Travelin'', and play the song (either the original on CD, or the recommended YouTube version). Ask students to read and listen, then ask for immediate reaction to words and music.
- Ask students to do Activity 3 individually, then check with a partner. (Answers: (a) he was travelling for work; the work was hard manual labour; (b) mining, harvesting, working in a steelworks; (c) by rail; on the road; (d) looking for a woman.)
- Ask for a quick, whole-class answer to this. (Answer: he was put in jail for 90 days for vagrancy – for which you might need to elicit/give the meaning: homelessness.)
- Activity 5 asks students to identify the way language is using which is American and song-specific. (Possible answers: putting *a-* in front of words (e.g. *a-havin'*, *a-hittin'*, *a-workin'*) is a way of making the words fit the rhythm of the line; missing the final *-g* from words (e.g. *pickin'*, d*umpin'*, *blastin'*) is a written reflection of what happens in colloquial speech and song; the use of *knowed* (instead of knew) to rhyme with *road*, but which also reflects rural/colloquial use; *travelin'* spelt with one *l* is the US form; the use of *hittin'* for *doing* is US usage; *it's sure been a-muckin'* is a US construction – in UK English we'd say *it's been really mucky.*)
- Activity 6 looks at the formal structure of the song. (Answer: it has seven four-line verses, with and AABC rhyme scheme, using the same words in each verse (*knowed-road*); there is an in-rhyme in the thirds line of each verse: *ramblin'-gamblin'*;*enders-cinders; suckin'-muckin'; hay-day; a-firin'-iron; said to me-vagrancy; mind-find* – these are true rhymes in verses 1, 3, 4, 6, 7 and half-rhymes in verses 2 and 5.)
- Activity 7 asks students to examine a possible purpose to the song, given that Guthrie was known to be a political writer. (Possible answer: in the American music traditions, traditional folk, blues and country songs often have the theme of the man 'going down the road', and so this may be taken as being a continuation of that tradition; however, given the reference to *a*

(continued on page 140)

TASK SHEET: **Hard travelling**

1. What do you understand by the phrase *hard travelling*? Give an example of what it would consist of. Have you ever done anything that you would consider to be *hard travelling*? Share your ideas with a partner.

2. Read the text and listen to the song 'Hard Travelin'' written by the American folk singer Woody Guthrie (1912–1967) in 1959.

3. Answer these questions about the content:
    a) What do verses 3–5 tell you about the reason for his travelling, and why it was *hard*?
    b) What three different types of work does he mention in verse 3–5?
    c) What different ways of travelling does he talk about in verses 2 and 7?
    d) In verse 7 he gives another reason for travelling around. What is it?
    Check your answers with a partner.

4. In verse 6 what happened to him and why?

5. Look at the language used in the song. Make a list of things which are different from the English that you would use, and explain them to a partner.

6. Describe the formal structure of the song. Check your ideas with a partner.

7. Woody Guthrie was well known as a politically committed writer and performer, but he also performed songs from the American folk tradition. Do you think this song has a message in it, and if so, what is it?

8. Compare this song with 'The Dalesman's Litany' (Lesson 2.3). In what ways is it the same and different?

dollar a day there might be some criticism of a system that pays a man poor wages for hard manual labour, which would agree with Guthrie's socialist viewpoint on life.)

Plenary (15 minutes): Do Activity 8 with the whole class if you have already done Lesson 2.3 with students; it would be interesting to compare the two songs. (Possible answers: In 'The Dalesman's Litany' (TDL) the singer leaves home because of and with his wife, and later children, and travels with her, while in 'Hard Travelin'' (HT) the singer doesn't have a woman; in both TDL and HT the singers do hard manual labouring work; TDL has a happy ending – they return to where they came from, while HT has no happy ending.

Homework: Ask students to find out more about Woody Guthrie and to come to the next class ready to share what they have found.

Differentiation: If you have some musicians in the class, ask them to get together and work up a version of 'Hard Travelin'' to perform to the other students. (Music tabs are available online.)

Truck rides

Introduction: The prose piece at the centre of this lesson was written in the USA in the same period as the song in Lesson 6.2, but describes a different type of *hard travelin'*, in that the protagonist chooses to leave home in order to get experience by hitching across the USA.

Aims and outcomes
- To read and enjoy a different viewpoint on the travelling theme
- To understand something of American culture

Resources required: Section 3, paragraphs 4–6 from Jack Kerouac (1957) *On The Road*. London: Penguin Books. This text is available online at:

 http://terebess.hu/english/ontheroad1.html

Lesson starter (15 minutes): Discuss with the whole class the pros and cons of hitchhiking, from the point of view of the hitcher and the driver. You could draw a table on the board, with four squares for: advantages/disadvantages, and hitcher/driver and complete it with student suggestions. Keep it abstract, so that the activity doesn't reduce the possibilities in Activity 1 of the main lesson.

Main lesson (35 minutes)
- Activity 1: Call back from the whole class some experiences, stories and comments.
- Activity 3. Students read the text and answer immediately; check quickly. (Answers: (a) he went to a place that was no good for hitching a ride; (b) he goes to where the petrol stations are and the trucks pass by; (c) the first driver indicates to another one behind to slow and pick him up; (d) having to talk to the drivers; (e) the cab of the second truck and a hotel in Des Moines.)
- Activity 4. (Answers: (a) treeless, grassy plains; (b) slowed the engine down; (c) a voice with a grating, harsh sound; (d) a big truck (US); (e) in a flash, in a moment; (f) to come into view indistinctly; (g) he drove very fast (US); (h) the engine sheds, often in an incomplete circle, with a turntable in the middle; (i) the worn out yellow blinds.)
- This looks at changes in feeling in the text. (Answers: at first he is unsuccessful, scared even, as it gets dark; then he tries something else, which is successful, and he's really happy when he easily gets his first ride; this feeling continues as he changes to the second truck; he feels strange in the car with the students after being in the trucks; finally in the shabby hotel he suddenly feels he has changed, he realizes he is on his way from childhood to manhood.)
- Activity 6 asks students to be sensitive to the tone of the writing. (Answers: the city places are shabby and negative – he's in a bus station, and when the second truck stops, he walks 'along the lonely brick walls illuminated by one lamp'; Des Moines is smokey; he stays in a 'gloomy old Plains inn of a hotel', in a shabby room by the railway roundhouse – note the negative adjectives used (*cracked high ceiling, beat yellow windowshades, dirty remarks carved in the wall, sad sounds*); although the future towns – Denver, San Francisco – seem positive. On the other hand the countryside is described positively: 'It was beautiful there . . . the purple darkness; the smell of the corn like dew in the night; like the Promised Land, way out there beneath the stars, across the prairie of Iowa and the plains of Nebraska.')

Plenary (10 minutes): Ask students to answer Activity 7 as a whole class activity. (Answer: it is the locations, and the trucks which make it feel American – the idea of huge trucks thundering through the night across thousands of miles of highway is very un-British)

Homework: Emphasize it is only the *events* they should summarize.

Differentiation: This comes through exposure to a different culture and time through the text.

TASK SHEET: **Truck rides**

1. Have you ever hitched a ride? If so, what was the situation, and what was it like? If not, why not? Do you know any stories about hitchhiking? Talk about your experiences and/or the stories in a group of four.

2. Read the extract from *On The Road*, a novel written by American author Jack Kerouac in 1957.

3. Answer these questions quickly:
   a) What mistake did the narrator make at first?
   b) What does he do the second time that is better?
   c) How does he get his second ride?
   d) What was the one thing he didn't like about hitchhiking?
   e) What two places did he sleep in?
   Check your answers with your group of four.

4. Look at the language used, and explain the meaning of these words and phrases:
   a) prairie
   b) cranked to a stop
   c) a hoarse raspy voice
   d) rig
   e) in the twink of nothing
   f) looming ahead
   g) he balled the jack
   h) the locomotive roundhouse
   i) the beat yellow windowshades
   Compare your answers in your group of four.

5. Explain how the narrator's feelings change from the beginning to the end of the extract and say why?

6. What general atmosphere is there about city places that are mentioned in this passage? How does the author achieve this? How do city places contrast with country places? Share your ideas with your group.

7. How American is this piece of writing? Justify your answer.

8. Summarize the *events* in this passage in a single paragraph of 75 words.

Which road will you take?

Introduction: Students read and unpick the meaning of this famous poem by Robert Frost.

Aims and outcomes
- To read, understand and enjoy a classic American poem
- To write a passage about choice and feelings post choice

Resources required: The poem 'The Road Not Taken' from Robert Frost (1916) *Mountain Interval*, found in Robert frost (1955) *Selected Poems*. Harmondsworth: Penguin. The poem is available online at:

www.poemhunter.com/poem/the-road-not-taken
http://en.wikipedia.org/wiki/The-Road_Not_Taken

Readings are listed on the website

Lesson starter (10 minutes): Ask students to tell you about their experiences of walking in the country.

Main lesson (40 minutes)
- Distribute the task sheets and ask students to think about, then discuss some choices they have made. Call back experiences from the whole class.
- Hand out/display Robert Frost's poem 'The Road Not Taken'. Ask the class to answer the two questions in Activity 3 immediately after reading the poem. (Answers: (a) Autumn (*yellow wood; leaves not step had trodden black*); (b) which road to go along when there was a fork in the path.)
- This activity requires careful and close attention in order to pick up what Frost actually says. (Answer: check words and phrases: *as just as fair*; *really about the same*; *equally lay* – in other words they were the same – one wasn't *less travelled by* – and his choice was random, without logic.)
- Activity 5 again requires close and careful attention to detail and thought about the dual meanings of the words *sigh* and *difference*. (Answers: (a) the future (i.e. something he cannot know); (b) a sigh of contentment, a sigh of regret; (c) a positive difference, a negative difference; (d) he didn't know anything – maybe in the future taking one path will have been the wrong choice, so a sigh of regret and negative difference; or maybe it will have been the right choice, so a sigh of contentment and positive difference . . . but until he lives his life he won't know, and so we don't know. (In another reading, it also could imply that whatever happens in the future he will always say that the path he chose was the *one less travelled by* [which is not the truth], sighing with contentment, because that sounds more exciting and adventurous.)
- The poem is very tight formally. (Answers: It has four 5-line verses, in an ABAAB rhyme-scheme, and with 9 (though occasionally 8 or 10) syllables per line.)

Plenary (10 minutes): Ask students what the point of this poem is. (Possible answer: to discuss how we see choices now, and how we might change them, or see them differently in the future.)

Homework: Ask students to do the writing Activity 7 for homework, using the start given (or allow them to start it in their own way if they prefer), and discussing their choice. They can use fantasy and imagination as much as they want.

Differentiation: The writing task allows for a great deal of personal freedom to write about what they feel and think.

TASK SHEET: Which road will you take?

1. Think about a time when you had to choose between two options (e.g. which of two laptops to buy; which of two parties to go to; which way to get somewhere). How did you decide? Was it rational and logical? Or was it a sudden feeling about one of the choices? Tell a partner about it.

2. Read the poem 'The Road Not Taken' by Robert Frost.

3. Answer these questions quickly:
   a) What time of year was it (say how you know)?
   b) What choice did the author have to make?

4. What do you find out about the two paths from verse 2 and the first two lines of verse 3? What was his logic for taking the 'other' path?

5. In order to understand the importance of the decision the writer made, read the final verse, and answer these questions:
   a) What time is he talking about in this verse?
   b) What two kinds of *sigh* are there?
   c) What two kinds of *difference* can something make on a person?
   d) What do the answers to these questions tell you about what the poet knew about his decision when he wrote the poem, and thus what we know about his decision?
   Discuss your ideas in a group of four.

6. Analyse the formal structure of the poem.

7. If you were in a 'yellow wood' and had to choose between two paths, one which was obviously well-used and the other which was 'less travelled by', which one would you choose, and why? Write 100–150 words on this theme, saying why it was better or worse to have taken the path you chose, what happened to you, whether you are pleased with your decision or regret not having taken the other path. Start like this: 'One sunny September morning I was walking through a yellow wood, and I came to a place where two roads diverged. I stood and looked at them both carefully. The one . . .'

In olden days

Introduction: This extract from one of the great European novels of the twentieth-century gives students a completely different perspective on the *On The Road* theme, both in period and culture.

Aims and outcomes
- To read and analyse a text from a different culture
- To think about the theme of travelling in a different period of history

Resources required: The extract from the opening of Chapter 2: Donnafugata from Giuseppe di Lampedusa (1958, trans 1960) *The Leopard*. London: Flamingo. Translated by Archibald Colquhoun (Resource Bank). Film details are given on the website.

Lesson starter (10 minutes): Ask students about Sicily (e.g. capital – Palermo; other cities; sights; location – south of Italy, near to Africa; landscape – bare, Etna; climate – hot, dry, especially in summer; produce – wine, olive oil, fish, oranges, fruit; the Mafia. Ask those students who have been to talk about it; if you have been and have suitable photos, contribute too.

Main lesson (40 minutes)
- Activity 1. (Answers: it was long, slow, difficult, dangerous; mostly by carriage [the rich], horse, horse-and-cart, stagecoach, on foot; roads unsurfaced, muddy, dusty, potholed; no good maps, no signs; risk of robbers; no superstructure [hotels, shops etc.]; badly affected by weather [hot, cold, wet]; very tiring.)
- Students read and answer Activity 3 immediately. (Answers: (a) carriage/horse; (b) heat/dust)
- Activity 4 analyses the description of the land. (Possible answers: *bare hillsides flaming yellow under the sun; crazed-looking villages; dry beds of torrents; Never a tree, never a drop of water; just sun and dust; the funereal countryside, yellow with stubble, black with burnt patches; the lament of cicadas filled the sky; parched.*)
- There is quite a lot of unusual, and possibly unknown vocabulary in this extract. Activity 5 asks students to find the meaning of 18 words/phrases; you may want to do this as a dictionary activity. (Answers: (a) flowed around; (b) the bells on the leather connections to the horses; (c) two wild plants; (d) to soften; (e) completely dried up; (f) smashed in; (g) made it go away; (h) spread the disease; (i) a book of psalms and prayers to be recited; (j) the fittest; (k) male servants; (l) smartness; (m) large neck-tie; (n) jokes, amusing comments; (o) beating corn to get out the grain; (p) insects which make a continuous whirring noise; (q) the noise someone makes in their throat just before they die; (r) the cut of lower stalks that remain in the field after harvesting, and are eventually burnt.)
- Activity 6. Vocabulary of horse movement. (Answers: *trot* is running along at a steady pace; *trudge* is working hard to keep moving; *shuffle* is going slowly, dragging your feet.)
- Activity 7. (Answers: (a) they are very tired, and all of them are dusty, because of the heat and the dust from the road; (b) he is smart and clean because he got there 30 minutes earlier and was able to clean himself up and relax a bit.)

Plenary (10 minutes): Ask the class to comment on the well (it's dangerous), the lunch (only rich people would have such a formal lunch), the farm (the broken leopard – symbol of the Salina family; the smashed door – decide if you want to bring up the Garibaldi unification of Italy issues against which the novel is set).

Homework: Ask students to write a modernized version of the journey.

Differentiation: The text is set in another country in other times.

1. What was travel like in the middle of the nineteenth-century? How did people get around? What problems did they face? Was there a difference between rich and poor? Discuss your ideas in a group of four.

2. Read the extract from *The Leopard* by Giuseppe di Lampedusa.

3. Answer these questions quickly:
    a) What two methods of transport are described?
    b) What are the two basic problems the travellers faced?

4. How is the land they pass through described? Note some examples and share them with your group.

5. Explain the following words and phrases:
a) *eddied back*	g) *It slaked thirst*	m) *cravat*
b) *harness bells*	h) *spread typhus*	n) *quips*
c) *sage and broom*	i) *breviary-reading*	o) *threshing*
d) *temper* (verb)	j) *spryest*	p) *cicadas*
e) *desiccated*	k) *lackeys*	q) *death-rattle*
f) *staved-in*	l) *spruceness*	r) *stubble*
    Check your answers in a group of four.

6. What is the difference between *trot, trudge* and *shuffle*? What makes these movements, when and why?

7. At the farmhouse:
    a) What state are many of the travellers in? Why?
    b) How is Tancredi different from all the others? Why?

8. The journey from Palermo to Donnafugata (in the province of Ragusa) is about 60 km (38 miles). In the extract it took them 5 hours to get to the farmhouse, then an hour or two for lunch, and there were two more hours to go. Imagine you are doing the trip today, in the same weather conditions, but in a modern air-conditioned car. Write 100–150 words describing your trip, and how you feel.

Riding with news

Introduction: This lesson works on Robert Browning's classic 'on the road' poem.

Aims and outcomes
- To introduce students to a famous poem from the canon of English Literature

Resources required: The poem 'How They Brought The Good News from Ghent to Aix' from Robert Browning (19045/1962) *The Poetical Works of Robert Browning*. London: Oxford University Press. This can be found online at:

http://bartelby.com/42/659.html
http://theotherpages.org/poems/brown01.html

Lesson starter (10 minutes): Ask students if any of them have ridden a horse, and get feedback from those with experience about what it's like; otherwise have students suggest what it's like based on watching films, horse races, etc.

Main lesson (40 minutes)
- Activity 1. Call back the answers from the whole class. (Answers: (a) stirrup: place to put a foot under a saddle; (b) gallop: the fastest movement of a horse; (c) saddle: the leather seat on a horse; (d) girth: the belt holding the saddle round the horse's body; (e) cheek-strap: leather belt on the horse's face; (f) bit: the metal bar that goes through a horse's mouth to control the reins; (g) spur: sharp spike on the rider's heel to make the horse go faster; (h) flank: the sides of the horse's body; (i) hanch: thighs; (j) chestnut colour of a horse; (k) back part; (l) = peak = projecting front part of the saddle.)
- Activity 3 looks at the story through time and place. (Answers: I: midnight – three riders leave Ghent; II: they ride; the narrator adjusts his saddle; III: dawn at Lockeren; morning star shows at Boom; Düffeld morning; Mechlen – 6 o'clock – they ride; IV: sun comes up; they pass cattle; V: about Roland's concentration; VI: Dirck's horse Roos collapses; VII: Midday – Joris and narrator riding; pass Looz, Tongres, Dalhem – they see Aix; VIII: Joris's horse collapses – narrator and Roland continue; IX: narrator gets rid of clothes to save weight, encourages his horse; they arrive at Aix; X: Friend appear, horse is given wine to revive him.)
- Activity 4 stresses the characters. (Answers: the unnamed narrator rides Roland; Dirck rides Roos; Joris rides an unnamed roan horse; Roland is the hero.)
- Activity 5 asks for supposition by students. (Possible answers: an attack has been called off, the enemy have been stopped . . .)
- Activity 6. Formal structure. (Answers: ten 6-line verses; AABBCC rhyme scheme; line length 11 syllables, with occasional 12-syllable lines; capitalisation to start each line; there is enjambment within verses, and across verses IV–V.)
- This activity looks at the vital element of rhythm which is what makes this poem work. (Answer: there are four beats per line, which generally work by starting on an unstressed word, or with two stressed words, and moving as follows (0=unstressed; /=stressed): 0/00/00/00/. It gives the poem its relentless forward 'riding' motion.)

Plenary (10 minutes): An opportunity for the whole class to express opinions about it – students typically find it an exciting, well executed poem.

Homework: Students locate the places mentioned on a map of Belgium, Holland and Germany.

Differentiation: The story is set in a different country in a different period of history.

TASK SHEET: **Riding with news**

1. You are going to read a famous poem about a horse-ride, so find out the meanings of these horse-related words first.

stirrup	gallop	saddle	girth
cheek-strap	bit	spur	flank
haunch	roan	croup	pique

Check your answers with a partner.

2. Read the poem 'How They Brought The Good News From Ghent To Aix' by Robert Browning, which he sets in the seventeenth-century.

3. Work with a partner. Complete the table, with brief notes about the content of each verse:

Verse	Time	Place	Action
I			
II			
III			
IV			
V			
VI			
VII			
VIII			
IX			
X			

4. What are the names of the riders and their horses? What happens to each horse during the ride? Who is the hero at the end?

5. What kind of *good news* do you imagine this was?

6. Describe the formal structure of the poem.

7. What can you say about the rhythmic nature of the poem?

8. What are your feelings about this poem?

9. Find a suitable map and mark the journey from Ghent (Gent, today) to Aix (Aachen today), with the other places mentioned.

A hard road

Introduction: In this lesson, students write about a difficult road journey – real or imagined.

Aims and outcomes

* To tell a story about a difficult road journey

Resources required: None.

Lesson starter (15 minutes): Ask students what, in general, can make travelling by road difficult. List their suggestions on the board. (e.g. weather conditions, the condition of the road itself, traffic, blockages, bandits, wild animals, the quality of your transport, your clothes, the terrain the road goes through . . .

Main lesson (40 minutes)

* Give out the task sheets, and ask students to start planning their journey by answering the five questions. Emphasize that they are travelling alone, and discuss any other points you feel need highlighting, such as the answer to (e) – summer, winter – will affect the problems they encounter.
* Ask them then to do Activity 2, where they decide on two major problems they face; again, discuss it with them if necessary, or draw their attention to the list you made in the Lesson starter; also remind them that the problems they face will be related to their answers to Activity 1.
* The five-part/five-paragraph plan is a convenient way of getting students to plan the action of their story. Refer them back to Lesson 6.6, and the Browning poem, in which the action is broken up by the time of the day and the towns they pass.

Plenary (5 minutes): Once they have planned their story and are ready to write it, draw students' attention to Activity 5, where they will find examples of the discourse markers necessary to structure their story-writing.

Homework (30 minutes in a subsequent lesson): Students write the first draft of their story for homework.

* They should bring it in to the next class, and do a peer correction exercise with a partner. They should read the story for clarity and organization, and suggest changes if it is difficult to follow. If they not any language errors as they read (e.g. wrong spelling, incorrect tense), they should underline the problem word(s) and leave the writer to decide what the problem is.
* They should then use the information from their partner to write a second version for you to read.

Differentiation: This will come out in their own experiences and the personal nature of the stories they write.

TASK SHEET: **A hard road**

1. Imagine that you have to make a difficult road journey by yourself from one place to another. Decide the following things, and note the details.
   a) Where you are going from? _____
   b) Where are you going to? _____
   c) Why are you going? _____
   d) How are you travelling? _____
   e) When does the journey take place? _____

2. Choose two major problems that you face in making this journey:
   a) _____
   b) _____

3. Divide the time that the journey takes into five periods (e.g. 5 hours, 5 days, from each of the five places to the next), and then work out what happens in each of those five periods; decide when in these five periods of time the two major problems occur.

4. Plan the outline for your story, called 'A Hard Road', using this framework:

Introduction (the information in 1) _____

Paragraph 1 _____

Paragraph 2 _____

Paragraph 3 _____

Paragraph 4 _____

Paragraph 5 _____

Conclusion _____

5. Make sure you sequence your story with the right discourse markers, for example: *first . . . then . . . next . . . after that . . . the following day . . . later on . . . in the evening . . . finally . . .*

Section 7   Places

A stone circle

Introduction: The first lesson in this section takes students to the prehistoric stone circle at Stanton Drew in Somerset, whose Great Circle, at 113 m in diameter, is the second largest in Britain after Avebury.

Aims and outcomes
* To read, analyse and appreciate a subtle contemporary poem

Resources required: The poem 'Stanton Drew' from U. A. Fanthorpe (1978) *Side Effects*. Calstock: Peterloo Poets, and also available in U. A. Fanthorpe (1986) *Selected Poems*. London: Penguin Books. You can find it online at:

 http://megalithicpoems.blogspot.com/2006_07_01_archive.html

Details of photos are on the website.

Lesson starter (10 minutes): Ask students what they think are the oldest human products to be found in Britain. Expect prehistoric tools, weapons, pots etc. If they don't give you 'stone circles', elicit them through a question such 'What about the oldest constructions?'

Main lesson (40 minutes)
* Give out the task sheets and ask students to do Activity 1 in a group of four. (Answers: expect things like: they were constructed around the sun and/or moon; Stonehenge, Avebury best known; date from BC 5000–1500; varied in size and level of workmanship on the stones; they are based on a standard measurement.) you may like to show students the pictures of Stanton Drew on the website cited above at this point.
* Hand out/display the poem 'Stanton Drew' by U. A. Fanthorpe and ask students to read it.
* Ask them to work through the questions as indicated, doing them individually, then discussing them with their partner. Call back some answers after they've done two or three questions to check they're on the right track.
* Activity 3 (Answer: she removes all the later additions to the landscape, to get back to what it was like in prehistoric times.); Activity 4 (Answer: grass, the Mendip Hills, the sky, the bare earth.); Activity 5 (Answer: the stones are the thing which gives meaning to the land; they are the only permanent man-made thing.); Activity 6 (Answer: cattle rubbing them, weather eroding them, archaeologists examining them.); Activity 7 (Answer: they are aligned to the sun at a particular time and place in winter, and the movements of the moon at other times – and many archaeologists believe stone circles were a kind of 'temple' to the sun/moon, or way of checking the year's cycle.); Activity 8 (Answer: you will feel connected to the past, feel its life.)
* This activity looks at the formal structure of the poem. (Answer: it is a single piece, 27 lines long; there is no rhyme/chime; the lines are from 5–11 syllables long, with 6 and 7 syllables being most frequent; each line starts with a capital letter.)
* This activity asks students to locate some images. (Answers: (a) *with its notches/Fresh, like carving*; (b) *Chain the moon's footsteps to/The pattern of their dance*; (c) *Over Maes Knoll's white cheek*.)

Plenary (10 minutes): Ask students what they think is the key point about the poem (Possible answer: the simple power of the ancient stones.)

Homework: Students write about a very old place they've been to and its connection to the past, and how they felt about it. It can be invented.

Differentiation: Students can deal with something real or imagined for homework.

TASK SHEET: **A stone circle**

1. Work in a group of four. Note down everything you know about prehistoric stone circles in Britain.

2. Read the poem 'Stanton Drew' by U. A. Fanthorpe.

Do all the following questions by yourself, but check your answers with a partner after each one.

3. Relate what is said in the first line to what the poet does in lines 2–8. Explain what is she doing.

4. What is the answer to the question 'What do you see now?' in lines 8/9? List the four things mentioned by line 14.

5. What does she imply about the stones in lines 14–18?

6. What three things does she say have changed the stones a little?

7. What two things does she say the stones do in lines 20–24? Based on what you know about stone circles in general, how does this relate to their original purpose?

8. What does she suggest will happen once you are inside the circle and touch one of the stones?

9. Describe the formal structure of the poem.

10. Find an example of (a) a simile (b) a metaphor and (c) personification.

In a Welsh slate mine

Introduction: This lesson offers another fine contemporary poem, this time by a Welsh poet, which explores the character of a different place.

Aims and outcomes

- To read, analyse and appreciate a contemporary poem

Resources required: The poem 'Slate Mine' from Gillian Clarke (1989) *Letting in the Rumour*. Manchester: Carcanet. Gillian Clarke is the National Poet of Wales. For background information *see* the website.

Lesson starter (10 minutes): Ask students what the roof of their house, and/or those around the school are covered with; ask what other things roofs can be made of or covered with (tiles, slate, thatch, wooden shingles, planks of wood, copper, concrete) and where the roofing products come from.

Main lesson (40 minutes)

- Hand out the task sheet and ask students to do Activity 1 in pairs. Call back answers from the whole class. (Possible answers: comes from quarries and mines in North Wales; it's a kind of stone which can be split into thin sheets; used for roofing, tombstones, kitchen surfaces, floor slabs, used to be used for writing on with chalk in schools.)
- Hand out/display the poem 'Slate Mine' by Gillian Clarke and ask students to read it. Ask students to do Activity 3 quickly and do a quick check with a partner before you call back answers from the whole class. (Answers: (a) false – the signs show this, and the rusting equipment; (b) true – she says *we*; (c) false – there are several gallery and *emptiness deep as cathedrals*; (d) true – ferns are growing and she can see a waterfall; (e) false – she 'feels' the presence of the earlier miners.)
- Activity 4 looks at some specific bits of language. (Answers: (a) the metal is dusty with rust like pollen on flowers; (b) they probably have to wade through ice-cold water to get in; (c) the spaces inside the mine are as empty and vast as all the space above you in a cathedral; (d) the slate is cutting through the untouched air – *panics* is a very unusual usage, indicating perhaps, her fear at the drop below, or the poet imagines that the disturbance causes panic for the stillness.)
- Activity 5 works on the overall feeling of place created. (Answer: she creates a sense of huge, untouched stillness, which echoes with the past strongly – the equipment used and the memories of miners, and also the sense of danger – the drops.)
- Activity 6 asks for structural analysis. (Answer: the poem has five four-line verses; there is no rhyme/chime scheme; line length varies from 4–11 syllables with no pattern – the rhythms follow natural speech; capitals are used only for the starts of sentences, which occur for each new verse, also for the three signs in verse 1.)
- This activity ask students to explain figures of speech. (Answers: (a) personification – the tops of ladders are human fingers; (b) metaphor – a stone (slate) cannot drown.)

Plenary (10 minutes): Discuss the atmosphere of the poem, and particularly elicit its connection to the past, and link this to the 'Stanton Drew' poem in Lesson 7.1; this by way of preparation for the homework.

Homework: Students write the essay in Activity 8 for homework.

Differentiation: Unless your class are from a Welsh slate-mining area, or from a mining area of another kind, this will deal with a very different kind of place and reality for them.

1. What do you know about slate? What is it? Where does it come from? What is it used for? Discuss your ideas in a pair.

2. Read the poem 'Slate Mine' by Gillian Clarke.

3. Answer these statements as true or false quickly:
   a) The slate mine is still used
   b) The poet visits the mine with at least one other person
   c) It is a small mine
   d) There is a little natural light in one place inside
   e) She finds the body of a dead miner
   Check your answers with a partner.

4. What do you understand by these phrases:
   a) *pollens of rust*
   b) *to the knees in ice*
   c) *emptiness deep as cathedrals*
   d) *my cast slate panics through generations of silence*
   Discuss your ideas with your partner.

5. What is the overall atmosphere of the mine which the poet gives?

6. Describe the formal structure of the poem.

7. What figures of speech are
   a) *Rungs crook rusted fingers over the drop*?
   b) *such a long wait/for the sound of drowning*

8. Write an essay on the following title:

    In 'Stanton Drew' and 'Slate Mine' both poets show a deep feeling for the past. Illustrate this with examples from the poems.

Peggotty's brother's house

Introduction: This lesson works on a famous description of place from Dickens, when David Copperfield first sees Peggotty's house. It is very different from the previous two lessons!

Main aims and objectives

- To read, enjoy and analyse a classic piece of English literature
- To write a detailed description of a room they know well

Resources required: The extract from Chapter 3 of Charles Dickens (1849/1994) *David Copperfield*. London: Penguin Popular Classics, page 35 (from ' Yon's our house, Mas'r Davy!') to page 37 (to 'where the pots and kettles were kept.') The text is available online at:

 www.online-literature.com/dickens/copperfield

Lesson starter (15 minutes): Ask students to examine the classroom, and describe it in detail, starting with shape, position and size of windows and door; then details of desks, tables and other furniture, lights and other fittings, then coming down to smaller features – maps, pictures on the wall, and so on; they should include colour and texture as appropriate.

Main lesson (35 minutes)

- Give out the task sheets and ask students to do Activity 1 in pairs.
- Give out/display the extract from *David Copperfield* by Charles Dickens, and ask students to read it.
- Ask them to complete the table in Activity 3 and then check with a partner. (Answers: (1) the work yards and such places they passed; (2) David examines the are – wilderness, sea, river, looking for Ham's house, but only sees an old boat; (3) David is enchanted by the boat as a house, describing the outside briefly, and discussing his feelings about it.)
- Activity 4 asks students to notice the details David notices, and categorize them. (Answers: furniture: dutch clock, chest of drawers, table, lockers and boxes used as chairs; crockery: cups, saucers, teapot; pictures: biblical scenes, the Sarah Jane; books: the Bible; ornaments: the painted teatray.)
- Activity 5 looks at vocabulary, and specifically asks students to link those which are connected to boats. (Answers: (a) littered with; (b) people who put tar between boat planks to make them waterproof; (c) a workman who rigs – puts the ropes on – a sailing boat; (d) a blacksmith's workshop, where metal is worked; (e) too old to be of use; (f) a mythical Persian bird; (g) home; (h) a wandering salesman; (i) the shelf structure over a fire; (j) the back of a boat; (k) to understand; (l) a small working sailing boat; (m) to make a little go a long way; (n) a small bunch of flowers; (o) a bed cover; (p) telling. Those connected to boats are: b – c – j – l.)
- A specific comprehension activity. (Answer: because it is *little* – his size.)
- A general comprehension activity. (Answer: he is delighted by it; he uses the positive adjectives: *romantic – wonderful charm – perfect abode – beautifully clean . . . tidy; completest and most desireable – delightful house.*)

Plenary (10 minutes): Ask students what they would like/dislike about living in such a place and why.

Homework: Students write a detailed description of a room; let them decide which room they choose, but insist it must be detailed and well organized.

Differentiation: Students are free to write about something they can personally respond to.

TASK SHEET: **Peggotty's brother's house**

1. Think about a room you know very well – your grandparent's sitting room, for example – and describe it in detail to a partner.

2. Read the extract from Charles Dickens' *David Copperfield*.

3. Look at the first three short paragraphs of description (ignoring the speech in between), and complete the table with brief notes about the contents of each:

Paragraph	Brief description of contents
1 (*Ham carrying – when Ham said:*)	
2 (*I looked – visible to me.*)	
3 (*If it had been – perfect abode.*)	

Compare your table with a partner.

4. List the objects in the fourth paragraph of description according to the headings:
   a) Furniture: _____

   b) Crockery: _____
   c) Pictures: _____
   d) Books: _____
   e) Ornaments: _____
   Check you list with a partner.

5. Check the meaning of the following words:
   a) *bestrewn*   g) *abode*   m) *eked out*
   b) *caulker*   h) *pedlar*   n) *nosegay*
   c) *rigger*   i) *mantel-shelf* o) *counterpane*
   d) *forge*   j) *stern*   p) *imparting*
   e) *superannuated* k) *divine* (verb)
   f) *roc*   l) *lugger*
   Which of these words are specifically connected to boats? Check your answers with a partner.

6. Why, in general, does David like his bedroom?

7. How does David feel about the whole house? Explain how you know.

8. Write a full and careful description of a room you know well – maybe the one you described in Activity 1.

A rococo room

Introduction: In this lesson we look at a completely different kind of room, and the surprising results on entering it.

Aims and outcomes
- To read, understand and enjoy a translated text from another culture (Hungarian)

Resources required: The extract from the chapter 'The Inheritance' from Magda Szabó (1987) *The Door*. London: Vintage. For details of rococo illustrations *see* the website.

Lesson starter (10 minutes): Ask students to describe what a room that has been completely shut up for a long time would be like.

Main lesson (40 minutes)
- Give out the task sheet and ask students to do Activity 1 in a group of four. Call back ideas and note their ideas on the board. This might be the time to let them skim the Wikipedia site referenced above and look at the pictures.
- Hand out/display the extract and ask students to read it. Ask the whole class to answer Activity 3 immediately. (Answer: everything in the room collapses into dust.)
- Activity 4 asks for a short written summary of the contents of the second paragraph.
- In Activity 5 students work on less familiar vocabulary by finding synonyms in the text. (Answers: (a) bequest; (b) salon; (c) aristocracy; (d) grasped; (e) chef d'oeuvre; (f) shattered; (g) pulverized; disintegrate.)
- Activity 6 asks students to look at 5 specific words connected with the room. (Answers: (a) painted in gold; (b) a design style from the early eighteenth-century; (c) a shelf/table/drawer system, usually in a corner, holding ornaments; (d) the padding in chairs; (e) a porcelain figure – a small statue.)
- This activity looks at a specific lexical set. (Answers: perished – disintegrate – tumbled down – crumbled into nothing – ruined – collapsed – splitting – bursting – turning to powder – broken – shattered – pulverized. Woodworm caused it to disintegrate. The effect is to show the totality of the destruction – nothing was saved.)
- Activity 8 asks students to work out the context of the story from the few clues that are given. (Answer: she was expecting a valuable inheritance; she left with nothing, because it all disintegrated to dust.)
- Activity 9 asks students to make a suggestion, based on the facts they read. (Answer: the Lieutenant Colonel came back for them, or someone else stole them because the door was left open.)

Plenary (10 minutes): Film is mentioned twice. Ask students whether they think this would make a good scene from a film, and why/why not.

Homework: Ask students to research about rococo style, and to come to the next class prepared to say something about it.

Differentiation: Activity 9 allows for different interpretations of the ending.

TASK SHEET: **A rococo room**

1. If you went into the recently-decorated sitting room of a rich person in 1730, what would it be like? What would you see in the way of furniture, furnishings, ornaments? What colours would the room be? Discuss your ideas in a group of four.

2. Read the extract from the chapter 'The Inheritance' from Magda Szabó's novel *The Door*.

3. In brief, what surprising thing happens in this extract?

4. Write a written description of the room as they see it at the beginning, in 30–40 words.

5. Find synonyms in the text for the following words:
   a) inheritance _____
   b) sitting room _____
   c) nobility _____
   d) held tight _____
   e) masterpiece _____
   f) broken into pieces _____
   g) turned into dust _____
   h) break into pieces _____
   Check you answers with a partner.

6. Explain what these words mean:
   a) gilded _____
   b) rococo _____
   c) console _____
   d) upholstery _____
   e) figurine _____
   Check your answers with a partner.

7. List all the verbs and verb phrases that are connected with destruction. What caused the destruction? What is the effect of all the verbs

8. What was the narrator expecting when she entered the room? What did she get in the end, and why?

9. What do you think happened to the clock and the figurines in the end?

At a country station

Introduction: In this lesson students work on the sense of place generated in one of the most famous and often anthologized poems, 'Adlestrop', about an unscheduled express-train stop at the village station, in the Gloucestershire countryside, near Moreton-in-Marsh.

Aims and outcomes
- To read, enjoy and analyse a classic twentieth-century poem

Resources required: The poem 'Adlestrop' from Edward Thomas (1994) *The Works of Edward Thomas*, Ware: Wordsworth Editions. Also available online at:

 www.poemhunter.com/poem/adlestrop
www.poetropical.co.uk/24.html

Lesson starter (10 minutes): Ask students to talk about their experience of travelling by train – try to elicit both positive and negative experiences.

Main lesson (40 minutes)
- Hand out the task sheets and ask students to work in groups of four to collect information about Gloucestershire. Call back what the groups have found, and list it on the board. (Possible answers: it is a rural, agricultural county, bordered by the River Severn. Capital city: Gloucester – famous cathedral, cheese, rugby team; Cheltenham – spa, football team; the Cotswold Hills – popular tourist destination; famous for Bourton-on-the Water (model village), Stow-on-the-Wold, Moreton-in-Marsh; many tiny villages, pretty old churches; also the Forest of Dean, beyond the Severn. Cheese-rolling. Berkeley Castle, Slimbridge Wildfowl Centre, Cotswold Water Park.)
- Distribute/display the poem 'Adlestrop' by Edward Thomas for students to read.
- Activity 3 asks students to understand the poet's reason for stopping. (Answer: the train stopped *unwontedly* – not as expected – and so he hadn't intended to stop there.)
- Activity 4 looks at the things Thomas mentions hearing and seeing. (Answers: he saw: the station sign with the name *Adlestrop* on it, and willow trees, willow-herb [a purple flower], grass, meadowsweet [a cream-coloured flower], and haycocks [small haystacks], small clouds; he heard: the steam hiss, someone cough, a blackbird singing, and other birds.)
- The three questions in Activity 5 are for quick whole-class answering. (Answers: (a) hot; (b) nothing – someone coughed . . . one got on or off the train – it was an unscheduled stop; (c) the countryside – flowers, grass haycocks, and the small clouds.) Note: the line 'No whit less still and lonely fair' often requires some explanation – you can 'translate' it as: 'not a bit less still or lonely or beautiful', or 'just as still and lonely and beautiful', meaning countryside and sky were equal.
- Activity 6 looks at the unusualness of the opening verse – almost unique in poetry; it alerts students to the fact of this through discussion of the *function* the language performs. You might take time to explain and exemplify the concept of *function* first if students are unfamiliar (for example, if you want to borrow somebody's pen, the language exponents for the request function depend upon how well you know the person you are asking: 'Have you got a pen?' might be good for a friend, but 'Excuse me, could I borrow your pen?' would be necessary for a stranger). (Answer: it is an answer to a question, such as: 'And do you remember any of the places you visited when you were in Gloucestershire?' or 'Do you know the village of Adlestrop?' – otherwise you can't start the poem with the word 'Yes', and

(continued on page 164)   162

TASK SHEET: **At a country station**

1. What do you know about Gloucestershire? What are the main towns and cities? What is the countryside like? What is it famous for? Work in a group of four to pool information.

2. Read the poem 'Adlestrop' by Edward Thomas.

3. Did the author intend to stop at Adlestrop? If so, why? If not, why did he stop there? What is the meaning of the word *unwontedly*?

4. Complete the table. While he was at Adlestrop station:

He saw	
He heard	

   Compare your answers with a partner.

5. Answer these questions quickly:
   a) What was the weather like?
   b) What did people do at the station?
   c) What two things were both *still and lonely*?

6. What language function does the opening verse of the poem from 'Yes' to 'Unwontedly' perform? Is it
   a) a request
   b) an order
   c) an answer
   d) a suggestion
   e) a refusal
   Explain the reason for your answer, and decide what would had to have gone before, for the opening to make sense. Why is this very unusual in poetry?

7. What atmosphere does the poet create in the closing verse of the poem?

8. Analyse the structure of the poem, then write up your description of it in 50–75 words.

'I remember Adlestrop'. Poems almost never start like this – they tend to work from inside themselves, not from the outside.)

Plenary (10 minutes)

- This activity asks students to sum up the important *sense* of the poem. Ask them to discuss it as a whole class. (Answer: it's an atmosphere of inclusion and belonging, everything united – the land, and sky, through the symbol of the bird's song, and how the poet feels connected to it.)

Homework: Students can work out the structure of the poem and write a 50–75 word descriptive analysis of it.

Differentiation: The world that is portrayed is one which has largely disappeared – the age of steam, the isolation of country places in the UK (though they can still be found elsewhere) – and so it will be a different world for most students to contemplate, not least the silence and stillness.

A cityscape

Introduction: To counterbalance the country scene of Lesson 7.5, this lesson looks at Wordsworth's famous and unexpectedly positive view of London.

Aims and outcomes
- To read, enjoy and analyse a classic poem from the canon of English Literature

Resources required: The poem 'Composed Upon Westminster Bridge, September 3, 1802' from Hutchinson T (Ed.) (1904) Wordsworth: Complete Poetical Works. Oxford: Oxford University Press. You can find it online at:

http://oldpoetry.com/opoem/5169-William-Worsworth-Composed-Upon-Westminster-Bridge--September-3--1802
http://theotherpages.org/poems/words01.html

and then scroll down through other Wordsworth poems. For information about readings *see* the website.

Lesson starter (5 minutes): Ask students what the difference between a city and a town is in general (cities are usually the administrative centre of a county or part of a county, often have a cathedral). Ask them what is meant by The City when applied to London (the central business, banking area, the old centre around St Paul's Cathedral).

Main lesson (50 minutes)
- Give out the task sheet and ask students to get into fours to discuss Activity 1. Call back answers from the whole class; you may want to note their suggestions on the board for later reference.
- Give out/display the poem and ask students to read it. Ask for answers to Activity 3 from the whole class quickly. (Answer: he's saying that on this morning London looked as beautiful as anything in the world.)
- Ask students to work through the poem answering the questions in Activity 4 individually, then check their answers with a partner. (Answers: (a) that this is the most beautiful sight on earth; (b) you would have to have no 'soul' to not appreciate the beauty; (c) the city is 'wearing' the beauty like someone would wear beautiful clothes . . . which gives the idea of it being temporary; (d) the city isn't closed and covered with smog, as usual, it's part of the beautiful natural world; (e) Wordsworth knows the city can be filthy, and invisible – he's a realist – but wants to show how beautiful it is when it's not like that; (f) that London looks as beautiful, and feels as calm, as any wild landscape in the early morning sun; *to steep* means to soak in; (g) the river [Thames] seems free, not dirty and abused by people; (h) the houses are usually 'alive' with people, about their business, but now even the buildings seem to be asleep; (i) London is a living heart – the heart of the 'body' of Britain.)
- Activity 5 asks students to get inside Wordsworth's mind as he looks at the capital, and see how the poem is something of a back-handed compliment. (Answer: the fact that this beautiful morning light is a *garment* – which can just as easily be taken off, the mention of *smokeless air* shows he knows what it's usually like, the use of *silent, calm, still* show that he knows that it's usually busy, noisy and full of action, the river flows at its *own sweet will* – no one is making it do things, like carry boats and goods and people; it's all a particular, special, unusual moment, and is a far cry from the daily reality of an overcrowded, squalid, dirty, industrialized city.)

(*continued on page 168*)

TASK SHEET: **A cityscape**

1. We often talk about a beautiful landscape, but is it possible to talk about a beautiful cityscape? Discuss how this might be beautiful in a group of four; list some examples.

2. Read the poem 'Composed Upon Westminster Bridge, September 3, 1802' by William Wordsworth.

3. In one simple sentence, what is Wordsworth saying in this poem?

4. Work through the poem answering these questions;
    a) What 'big' statement does he make in the first line?
    b) In lines 2–3 he talks about people's attitude to what he is looking at; what does he say about it?
    c) What simile do you find in lines 4–5? What is its effect?
    d) In lines 5–7, what is the significance of the word *Open*?
    e) What is important about the word *smokeless* in line 8?
    f) Given that Wordsworth comes from the Lake District and writes poems about the beauty of nature, what is surprising about lines 9–11? What does the verb *steep* mean?
    g) What does line 12 imply about the river? What river is it?
    h) He seems surprised in line 13. Why?
    i) What metaphor does he use for London in line 14?
    Check your answers with a partner.

5. In what ways does Wordsworth show that he is a realist about the true nature of London?

6. Analyse the formal structure of the poem.

7. What do you think Wordsworth was trying to say in this poem?

8. Practise the poem so that you can read it, or say it by heart, with the right expression, and be prepared to perform it for others.

- In Activity 6 students analyse the form, which is very tight. (Answer: it is a Petrarchan sonnet, with an ABBAABBA octave, and an EFEFEF sestet making up its 14 lines; there are 10 syllables per line, although in line 8, he should have written *glittering* as 'glitt'ring' to make it 2 syllables as it's usually said, not 3 syllables as it really is (as he does to change the 2 syllable *never* in line 9 into the 1 syllable *ne'er* in line 11); he uses initial capitalization in each line; several sentences run from one line to the next, however he only fully stops line (with a colon, semi-colon or full-stop) at the ends of lines.

Plenary (5 minutes): Ask students to answer Activity 7 as a whole class. (Answer: he shows that even as unnatural a phenomenon as London can look romantic, natural and beautiful without human activity destroying it.)

Homework: Practice saying it to make it sound correct. Prepare to perform it for others.

Differentiation: The poem asks students to look at something they're familiar with (the city of London) but from a different time and perspective.

My favourite place

Introduction: In this lesson the students write a description of their favourite place.

Aims and outcomes
- To write an authentic personal composition about their favourite place

Resources required: None.

Lesson starter (10 minutes): Asks students to tell a partner what the best place they've ever been to is, and explain why it's the best. Call back answers, with partners telling about each other.

Main lesson (40 minutes)
- Hand out the task sheet, and ask students to choose and note down a favourite place that they are going to write about in Activity 1.
- Activity 2 helps students to start to get inside their feelings about their place, by noting down what things about it affect which senses.
- Activities 3–5 ask them to note down any people, objects or other things (e.g. animals, events which occurred there) they associate with the place.
- Activity 6 works on their emotional response to being at their place, or away from it.

Plenary (10 minutes): Activity 7 gives students a framework on which to hang their description of 'my favourite place'. Talk through the framework.

Homework (30 minutes in a subsequent lesson): Students use the framework to write a first draft of their description.
- When they have finished, they should work in a pair for peer correction. Partners should check each other's description for clarity and organization, and point out any problems there are in that regard. If they also notice any language errors (e.g. spelling mistakes, wrong tense) they should underline these and leave the writer to check and correct them.
- They should then write a second draft, which can be handed in to you to read.

Differentiation: This is a flexible activity which gives all students room to move inside it.

My favourite place

Introduction: In this lesson the students write a description of their favourite place.

Aims and outcomes
* To write an authentic personal composition about their favourite place

Resources required: None.

Lesson starter (10 minutes): Asks students to tell a partner what the best place they've ever been to is, and explain why it's the best. Call back answers, with partners telling about each other.

Main lesson (40 minutes)
* Hand out the task sheet, and ask students to choose and note down a favourite place that they are going to write about in Activity 1.
* Activity 2 helps students to start to get inside their feelings about their place, by noting down what things about it affect which senses.
* Activities 3–5 ask them to note down any people, objects or other things (e.g. animals, events which occurred there) they associate with the place.
* Activity 6 works on their emotional response to being at their place, or away from it.

Plenary (10 minutes): Activity 7 gives students a framework on which to hang their description of 'my favourite place'. Talk through the framework.

Homework (30 minutes in a subsequent lesson): Students use the framework to write a first draft of their description.
* When they have finished, they should work in a pair for peer correction. Partners should check each other's description for clarity and organization, and point out any problems there are in that regard. If they also notice any language errors (e.g. spelling mistakes, wrong tense) they should underline these and leave the writer to check and correct them.
* They should then write a second draft, which can be handed in to you to read.

Differentiation: This is a flexible activity which gives all students room to move inside it.

TASK SHEET: **My favourite place**

1. What is your favourite place? If you have two or three, choose one of them at random. Write down exactly where it is:

2. Note down things you remember about it, related to the five senses:
   a) sight:
   b) smell:
   c) taste:
   d) sound:
   e) touch:

3. What people do you associate with it, if any:

4. What objects do you associate with it, if any:

5. Anything else that's special about this place for you:

6. Write down some adjectives to describe how you feel when you're there:

   and how you feel when you're not there:

7. Now plan your description using the framework below:

Title: My Favourite Place
Paragraph 1:   Introduction/details of the location (in Activity 1)
Paragraph 2:   detailed physical description of the whole place (in Activities 2–5)
Paragraph 3:   information about when you first went there/how often you go
Paragraph 4:   your personal feelings about the place, and the reasons for that (in Activity 6)
Paragraph 5:   Conclusion, summing up the place and your feelings

Section 8　Strange Stories

Catching a bus

Introduction: This lesson looks at a poem which starts with something most people have done – run for the bus – but ends with it turning into a wild adventure, before returning to a banal ending.

Aims and outcomes

- To read, analyse and enjoy an imaginative contemporary poem

Resources required: The poem 'The Last Bus To Nowhere' from Neil Rollinson (1996) *A Spillage of Mercury.* London: Cape Poetry (Resource Bank).

Lesson starter (10 minutes): Ask students about which types of public transport they've used (bus, train, tram, trolley bus, coach, underground), which they prefer, and why.

Main lesson (40 minutes)

- Students do Activity 1 and 2 together, in pairs. Call back experiences from the whole class, having one student tell the class about their partner.
- Activity 4. Students read the text and answer quickly. (Answers: (a) the sort of double-decker with a pole and a platform at the back left-hand side; (b) he sprints, and gets hold of the pole; (c) he is pulled along by the bus; (d) with great effort he pulls his knees up onto the platform.)
- Activity 5 works on some of the vocabulary in the poem. (Answers: (a) as fast as possible; (b) an old hand-held flickering kind of film, where you can't see everything; (c) there was still no definite result – it could go either way; (d) a sudden violent movement; (e) waved around wildly; (f) the strip of material hanging at the back of a vehicle that releases electric charges which build up through motion; (g) a bad dive into the water, where the diver comes painfully down flat on their stomach; (h) the fast shallow areas of water in a river, usually littered with rocks.)
- Students make their own minds up about the answer to Activity 6. Ask it as a whole-class question, and elicit responses and discussion. (Answers: probably, in real life he would fall down; it's not really a possible scenario.)
- Activity 7 asks for analysis of what the writer says at the start. (Answer: *something snapped* and he decided to go for it, even though it was unnecessary – a sudden impulse.)
- Activity 8 asks for analysis of what the writer describes. (Answer: it's very calm, although you might have expected someone to notice the writer's situation and come to help him.)
- Activity 9 asks for analysis of the form of this irregular poem. (Answer: there are 41 coninuous lines; there is no rhyme/chime scheme; line length varies from 4–11 syllables with 7 and 8 syllables being most frequent; initial word capitalization is only used for lines where new sentences start; there is enjambment throughout.
- Activity 10 asks students to locate figures of speech. (Answers: there are 5 similes: *like Super-8 Film; like an earthing-strip; (like) a diver in mid belly-flop; as calm as somebody's sitting room; rushed under me like rapids.*)

Plenary (time depends on the number of performances): Students perform the poem for each other.

Homework: Ask students to prepare to perform the poem so as to bring out the energy, movement and excitement of the story.

Differentiation: The first two activities allow students to bring a lot of their own personal experience into play.

TASK SHEET: **Catching a bus**

1. Do you use buses to get around? How often? What journeys? When was the last time you used a bus? Do you like using buses? Why/why not? Talk to a partner about this.

2. Have you ever been late for a bus, and had to run for it, or just missed it, or just caught it? Describe one or more situations like this you have been in to your partner.

3. Read the poem 'The Last Bus to Nowhere' by Neil Rollinson.

4. Answer these questions quickly:
    a) What kind of bus is it?
    b) How does the writer catch it?
    c) What happens to him after that?
    d) How does he get onto the bus?
    Check your answers with a partner.

5. What do these words and phrases mean?
    a) *full tilt*
    b) *Super-8 film*
    c) *touch and go*
    d) *lurched*
    e) *flailed*
    f) *an earthing-strip*
    g) *belly-flop*
    h) *rapids*
    Check with a partner.

6. How possible is what happens in this poem? What do you think would happen in real life?

7. What do you understand about the writer's reasons for chasing the bus?

8. What is unusual about the inside of the bus?

9. Describe the formal structure of the poem.

10. What examples of figures of speech (e.g. metaphor, simile) can you find?

11. Perform the poem in such a way as to bring it to life.

Aliens!

Introduction: This famous poem takes the adage that 'poetry should make the familiar strange' as its purpose, looking at everyday objects and actions from a Martian's point of view.

Aims and outcomes
- To read, analyse and enjoy a famous contemporary poem
- To write some examples of their own on the same basis

Resources required: The poem 'A Martian Sends a Postcard Home' from Craig Raine (1979) *A Martian Sends a Postcard Home*. Oxford: Oxford University Press. It is online at:

 www.poetryconnection.net/poets/Craig_Raine/2568
http://plagiarist.com/poetry/2627

Lesson starter (10 minutes): Ask students what they know about the planet Mars – where it is (fourth planet from the Sun – our 'outside neighbour', what its surface is like (red rock), what has been found out about it (it may hold water as ice) and any other information.

Main lesson (40 minutes)
- Activity 1. Elicit opinions and encourage reasoned whole class discussion.
- Activity 2. Again, encourage opinions and ideas from the whole class.
- Ask students what people typically write on postcards home, then ask what they think a Martian might write on a postcard home from Earth.
- Activity 4. Students read the poem and work out what the eight things mentioned in it are. Call back answers and list them on the board. (Answers: (1) books [verses 1–3]; (2) mist [verses 4–5]; (3) rain [verse 6]; (4) car [verses 7–8]; (5) watch/clock [verse 9]; (6) phone [verses 10–12]; (7) going to the toilet [defecation] [verses 13–15]; (8) dream [verses 16–17].
- Activity 5 works on specific phrases the Martian uses. (Answers: (a) cry; (b) laugh; (c) ignition; (d) the phone rings; (e) dialling a number; (f) sleep in bed.)
- Activity 6 asks students to explain longer phrases. (Answers: (a) looking through mist is like looking at a black-and-white picture through tissue paper; (b) only children are allowed to defecate in public [into a potty]; (c) when it is dark.)
- Activity 7. Figures of speech. (Answers: they are mostly metaphors; other examples are *Model T is a room with the lock inside; Rain is when the earth is television; Mist is when the sky is tired.* The only other figure of speech is the simile *like engravings under tissue paper.)*
- The poem has a very limited formal structure. (Answer: there are 17 two-line verses (couplets); there is no rhyme/chime scheme, (although lines 1–2, and 16–17 rhyme incidentally); line length varies from 4–12 syllables, randomly; initial capitalization is only used for starting sentences; enjambment occurs within and across couplets.)

Plenary (10 minutes): Ask students to discuss what they think of the ways the Martian sees the objects he describes. Is that really how an alien might view them?

Homework: Ask students to think up a few 'Martian' views of everyday things of their own; they should write them on separate pieces of paper and bring them to class to hand around for others to guess what they are.

Differentiation: This poem is a fine example of differentiation, making us look at everyday things from a different perspective; the writing activity allows students to invent their own Martian views of Earth.

TASK SHEET: **Aliens!**

1. What is your opinion about UFOs and aliens? Do you think they exist? Have aliens actually landed on Earth? Collect your ideas and then discuss them in a group of four.

2. If aliens came to Earth, they would have to have extremely advanced technology. What things on Earth do you think they would find particularly strange or 'old-fashioned'? Discuss your ideas in your group.

3. Read the poem 'A Martian Sends A Postcard Home' by Craig Raine.

4. In the poem the Martian tries to explain eight of the things it has seen on Earth. Write the things it describes, and the numbers (1–17) of the verses:
   1) _____ (verses 1–3)
   2) _____ (_____)
   3) _____ (_____)
   4) _____ (_____)
   5) _____ (_____)
   6) _____ (_____)
   7) _____ (_____)
   8) _____ (_____)
   Check your answers with a partner.

5. 'Translate' these actions and things into 'normal' English:
   a) *the eyes melt* _____
   b) *shriek without pain* _____
   c) *the lock inside* _____
   d) *the ghost cries* _____
   e) *tickling with a finger* _____
   f) *they hide in pairs* _____
   Check your answers with a partner.

6. Explain what is meant by these parts of the 'postcard home':
   a) *like engravings under tissue paper* (verse 5)
   b) *only the young are allowed to suffer openly* (verse 12)
   c) *when all the colours die* (verse 16)
   Compare your answers with a partner.

7. Most of these statements, like 'Caxtons are mechanical birds' are examples of which figure of speech? What other ones can you find like this? There is one example of another figure of speech in the poem; what is it?

8. Analyse the formal structure of the poem.

9. Invent some examples of your own about other pieces of equipment or human behaviour that the Martian might have written home about.

She did what?!

Introduction: In this lesson, students deal with a poem about a person who becomes a goat.

Aims and outcomes
- To read, enjoy and analyse a contemporary poem
- To write a piece of poetry or prose in response to it

Resources required: The poem 'Goat' from Jo Shapcott (1992) *Phrase Book*. Oxford: Oxford University Press. It is available online at:

www.timesonline.co.uk/tol/life_and_style/article624914.ece

Lesson starter (10 minutes): Ask students to work in pairs and make a list of farmyard animals and birds. Elicit these from the students and write them on the board; elicit and include goat if it hasn't come up. Ask them which they like most/least and why.

Main lesson (40 minutes)
- Give out the task sheets and ask students to get into fours to brainstorm goats; they should make notes. Call back everything they give you and list it on the board, maybe under headings (e.g. physical, diet, produce, character, connotations . . .)
- Hand out/display the poem and ask students to read it. Ask for an immediate whole-class response to Activity 3. (Answer: she was walking down the road and she changed into a goat.)
- In Activity 4 students are asked to analyse the four content areas of the poem. (Answers: [1–8] the physical change from human to goat; [9–16] what she likes about being a goat; [16–21] enjoying what she could smell; [21–30] eating everything.)
- Activities 5–6–7 all ask for closer analysis of the sections outlined in Activity 4. Students can do these, then check with a partner before you call back the answers from the class. (Answers: Activity 5: horns, spine, hoofs; Activity 6: being close to other bodies; Activity 7: earth, grass, leaves, twigs, flowers, beer cans, condoms.)
- Activity 8 looks closely at the 'difficult' last section and asks students to create meaning out of it. (Answers: goats are known to eat 'everything' – but here this includes the sun, the clouds and buildings, one of which has a human in it; this may (!) indicate the insignificance of humans for goats, or be a dig at human self-importance . . .)
- In Activity 9 students analyse the structure of the poem. (Answers: free verse; 30 lines long; no rhyme/chime scheme, random rhymes/chimes (*go/glue, ear/here; wanted/world;clouds/town*); line length varies from 8–14 syllables, with 11 being most frequent; initial capitalization only for new sentences; enjambment.)

Plenary (10 minutes): Given the strangeness of this poem, it would be a good idea to round up with a whole-class discussion of it, eliciting feelings about it.

Homework: Students use this idea of changing into an animal and make it their own. The task sheet suggests farm animal or a pet, but if students have some other animal in mind, then they should be encouraged to use it.

Differentiation: The homework allows students to express their individuality.

TASK SHEET: She did what?!

1. What do you know about goats? Work in a group of four and pool your knowledge.

2. Read the poem 'Goat' by Jo Shapcott.

3. In as few words as possible, what is the basic 'fact' of this poem ?

4. Read the poem again and make very brief notes in the table on the four areas of content to be found in the poem.

Lines of poem	Content
Lines 1–8	
Lines 9–16	
Lines 16–21	
Lines 21–30	

Compare your answers in your group of four.

5. What three physical changes does the poet note?

6. What does she like about being with goats that she doesn't like about being with humans?

7. What things can she smell?

8. What do you understand by the last section (lines 21–30)? And what, in particular, is the significance of the last four lines?

9. Analyse the formal structure of the poem.

10. What is your overall feeling about this poem?

11. Write a poem or a piece of prose where you change into some type of domestic animal – a farm animal, or a pet; structure your writing carefully into different areas of the experience, starting, like this poem, with the nature of the physical change.

Talking to her teeth?

Introduction: This lesson asks students to read and analyse another contemporary poem with a strange, sad story to it, which they need to unpick.

Aims and outcomes

- To read, enjoy and analyse a contemporary British poem

Resources required: The poem 'The Woman Who Talked To Her Teeth' from Vicki Feaver (2006) *The Book of Blood*. London: Cape Poetry. It can be found by searching online at:

 www.google.com

Lesson starter (10 minutes): Ask students to discuss the advantages/disadvantages of having all your teeth out at 18; list their ideas on the board in two columns.

Main lesson (45 minutes)

- Give out the task sheets and ask students to do Activity 1 in pairs. Call back some experiences and feelings in a whole-class setting.
- Give out/display the poem 'The Woman Who Talked To Her Teeth' by Vicki Feaver and ask students to read it.
- Ask them to work through the questions in Activity 3 individually, then check their answers with a partner. There are no problem vocabulary issues in this poem. (Answers: (a) to save money, and time once they had families; (b) she was unattractive because of the scar, and was 'left out', never married; (c) soft food which didn't require chewing – because she didn't use her false teeth [or never had them made]; (d) could be relatives, friends, neighbours – people who would want to celebrate her sixtieth birthday – or, more sadly, the nurses in the mental hospital where she lived [this depends on your reading of 'the grass' and actions in the final two verses]; (e) too obviously he back lawn . . . possibly the lawns of the mental institution where she lives; (f) very sad – a wasted life, the teeth a symbol of her unfulfilled teenage aspirations for home and family; (g) they smile at her, she's afraid of them.)
- Activity 4 asks students to look for facts. (Answers: she had her teeth out in her teens; she expected to get married and have children; she was unattractive [facial dog bite scar]; she never married, never had much social life; she didn't use her false teeth; she ate soft food; she lived until at least 60; there was to be a party; she told her teeth stories.)
- Activity 5 asks students to get behind the facts of Activity 4 and imagine this woman's life. (Answers: will be largely subjective and speculative . . . but one can't help feel that she lives in an institution; friendless, unattractive, not using teeth, mouth shut – no communication . . .)
- This asks for formal analysis of the poem. (Answers: six 5-line verses; no rhyme-chime scheme; line-length varies from 5–11 syllables, with 6 syllables most frequent; initial capitalization is only for the start of sentences; all new sentences begin at the start of a new line; no inter-verse enjambment, but inside verses lines run on.)

Plenary (5 minutes): Ask students to comment about the feelings the poem generates.

Homework: The written assignment asks students to reflect on the way that the simple, flat, matter-of-fact way the story is told heightens the emptiness and sadness of the main character's life, as revealed in the final two verses.

Differentiation: Students can put their own 'spin' on the story; they also have opportunities to discuss their own ideas and experiences in the Lesson starter and Activity 1.

TASK SHEET: Talking to her teeth?

1. When was the last time you went to the dentist and what did you go for? No one likes going to the dentist's, but are you okay about going, or does it make you nervous? How often do you go? What's your dentist like? What don't you like about visiting the dentist? Discuss your feelings and experiences with a partner.

2. Read the poem 'The Woman Who Talked To Her Teeth' by Vicki Feaver.

3. Answer the questions about each verse.
   a) Verse 1: Why did *lots of girls* have their teeth out in their teens?
   b) Verse 2: What does this verse tell you about the main character's life?
   c) Verse 3: What sort of food did she eat, and why?
   d) Verse 4: Who are *They*? What 3 things did she get for her sixtieth birthday?
   e) Verse 5: Where was *the grass*?
   f) Verse 6: What is the feeling in this final verse?
   g) Verse 5/6: What two contrasting attitudes does the main character show towards her new false teeth?

   Check you answers with a partner.

4. What information do we actually find out about the main character in this poem? Tell a partner.

5. What things do you imagine about the main character, based on what is said in the poem?

6. Analyse and describe the structure of the poem.

7. 'This poem is written in deceptively simple language, which makes the ending even sadder.' Explain this statement, with examples from the poem in 140–160 words.

Introduction: This lesson uses a poem describing a peculiar incident at a railway station in Exeter.

Aims and outcomes
- To read, enjoy and analyse a contemporary poem
- Students act out the scene described in the poem

Resources required: The poem 'Incident in Exeter Station' from Matthew Sweeney (2000) *A Smell of Fish*. London: Cape Poetry. It is also available online at:

 www.guardian.co.uk/books/2000/feb/26/poetry.features1

Lesson starter (10 minutes): Ask students to describe a typical railway station – what does it look like, what buildings does it have, what signs, people, announcements, machines are there.

Main lesson (40 minutes)
- Activity 1. Call back reactions from the whole class.
- Activities 3 and 4. Examining the two main characters. (Answers: 3: he's having a drink in the station bar/restaurant whilst waiting for his train – perhaps sitting on one of the high stools in front of the bar; 4: the man is a stranger, with a duffel bag, thin face, dirty, uncut hair; he chooses the narrator as his victim to 'attack', maybe just wanting company, maybe a free drink; perhaps he's somewhat deranged, homeless . . . there's room for student speculation here.)
- Activity 5. Key language elements. (Answers: (a) the poem starts dramatically, introducing the unknown characters *He* and *me* and the action *came in the door* and the relationship *looking like he'd known me in another life* – which sets up the doubt of whether the *he* did know the *me* – a tension; (b) the man is intense, making strong eye contact; (c) one of sadness and knowing – he'd expected this; (d) it contorted into something frightening, inhuman – with all the dangerous and evil overtones that *voodoo* carries with it; (e) he feels ashamed of being associated with this man by the public; (f) he sees a way out – a train – and rushes onto it, regardless of where it's going, just to escape the situation; (g) he's afraid to go back in case he meets the man again, or perhaps because others will associate him with the man.)
- Activity 6. Examining sentence structure. (Answers: first half – eight short sentences; second half – one long sentence. This shows the series of events, at first separate, the narrator perhaps trying to ignore them, hoping he can escape the man's attention, not wanting to be connected to him; these lead like steps up to the final action, which, in the narrator's mind, is a single sequence, from the stranger's changing face through the shouting and his escape to the narrator on an unknown train facing the future. It's a very good example of sentence structure following and indicating the plot.)
- Activity 7 is a formal analysis of the poem's structure. (Answer: the poem has 29 lines, without rhyme/chime – free verse; the lines are from 7–11 syllables long, with 8 and 9 syllables being most frequent; initial capitalization goes with the sentence structure; the lines run on.)
- Activity 8. Students work in threes; they can perform for others, and the performances can be discussed, saying what was good, what could be improved and how.

Plenary (10 minutes): Discuss student views of the man – who he was and what his problem was.

Homework: A brief summary, reducing 203 words to 25–30, to capture the poem's essence.

Differentiation: This poem exploits differentiation in terms of people's different public behaviour and the reactions to it, thereby allowing students to consider how we are all different in some way.

TASK SHEET: **Why did he do that?**

1. Imagine you are standing somewhere in public – in a bus queue, at the supermarket checkout, for example – and someone you've never seen before comes up to you and starts talking to you as if they know you, calling you by a name that isn't yours, talking about things you've done together, asking questions about your brother . . . What would you do? Discuss this situation with a partner.

2. Read the poem 'Incident in Exeter Station' by Matthew Sweeney.

3. Where is the narrator and what is he doing when the *incident* happens?

4. What facts do you find out about the man who talks to the narrator. What other things can you suppose about him? Discuss your ideas with a partner.

5. Explain these things to a partner:
   a) The impact of the first two lines
   b) The significance of line 10 (*he looked into my eyes like a holy man*)
   c) The sort of smile the man gave the narrator, given the comparison that is made
   d) How the man's face changed, in order to become *a voodoo mask*
   e) The narrator's feelings in line 22 (*but I knew they classed us together*)
   f) The significance of the narrator's leaving (lines 23–26)
   g) The author's current relationship with Devon

6. Examine the sentence structure of the poem, comparing what happens from lines 1–15 (to *ever seen you before.*), and then from lines 15 (*He smiled*) to the end. What is the effect of this?

7. Analyse the formal structure of the poem.

8. Work in a group of three. One of you is the reader, one the narrator, the other the stranger. Work out an acted version of the poem; the reader should read everything in the poem, except the words the narrator and the stranger actually say; the narrator and the stranger should act out the parts, moving as appropriate, so set up a space as you think it should be.

9. Write a summary of the poem in 25–30 words.

Comparing character portrayal

Introduction: This lesson is intended for students who have already worked through Lessons 8.4 and 8.5, as it works on the two poems studied there. However, it could also be used as a 'blind' exercise, for students to compare two unseen texts on their own, especially given that there is no difficult vocabulary or structural issues with either poem.

Aims and outcomes

- To write a comparative essay about the characterisation of the people in the poems 'The Woman Who Talked To Her Teeth' by Vicki Feaver and 'Incident in Exeter Station' by Matthew Sweeney.

Resources required: *See* the Resources needed sections of Lessons 8.4 and 8.5 to know how to find the necessary texts.

Lesson starter (10 minutes): Discuss aspects of characterisation with the students. Elicit/tell the students that while writers may tell the reader about particular actions a character performs, and give us opinions about them from third parties, the best writing shows us what people are like through the things they say and/or do, and leaves the reader to make up their own minds about them.

Main lesson (50 minutes)

- Decide how you want to organize this Lesson. It could be a simple class writing activity, a timed writing 'test', or done for homework. Alternatively you could make it into a pair-writing activity where two students work on one composition together, with discussion about organization and content.
- Provide students with copies of the two poems ('The Woman Who Talked To Her Teeth' by Vicki Feaver and 'Incident in Exeter Station' by Matthew Sweeney), and a copy of the task sheet.
- Ask them to read the task sheet carefully, as the points raised in 2 and 3 should form the basis of their writing.
- Ask them to read the title carefully before they start. Remind them that they should plan the organization of their writing before they actually start writing.
- Depending on how you decided to organize the lesson, you may wish to have a different outcome. Decide if you want peer correction (Of organization? Content? Language? Or all three elements?) and then redrafting before it is handed in to you. Or whether it is a 'test' that comes directly to you.

Plenary (timing will depend on how you organize this and the numbers of students): Students read and discuss each other's writing.

Homework: Students write their own description of a real or imagined 'strange' person, either as a poem or as a paragraph of prose.

Differentiation: Students explore differences in people, individually, with original writing.

TASK SHEET: **Comparing character portrayal**

1. Read the two poems 'The Woman Who Talked To Her Teeth' by Vicki Feaver and 'Incident in Exeter Station' by Matthew Sweeney.

2. Pay special attention to the way that the poets portray the main characters (the *She* of the Vicki Feaver poem and the *He* of the Matthew Sweeney poem). Think carefully about:
   a) What they tell us about the characters
   b) What they don't tell us about them
   c) What actions they are shown doing
   d) What we are left to decide for ourselves about the situation

3. Notice, too, the language of the poem and how this affects the feelings we get about the two characters.

4. Now write an essay on the following topic:

   The poems 'The Woman Who Talked To Her Teeth' by Vicki Feaver and 'Incident in Exeter Station' by Matthew Sweeney both introduce characters whose behaviour is disturbing. Compare the ways in which the two poets handle the characters, through what they tell and show us, and the language they use.

   Use 400 words.

A hut and an old lady

Introduction: This lesson works on the analysis of a New Zealand short short story.

Aims and outcomes
* To read and enjoy a short story from a different culture, with a 'spooky' twist
* To write an analysis of the structure of the story

Resources required: The short short story 'The Bach' by Patricia Donnelly from Graham Lay (Ed.) (1997) *One Hundred New Zealand Short Short Stories*. North Shore City: Tandem Press (Resource Bank).

Lesson starter (10 minutes): Ask students to tell you whatever information they can about New Zealand – places, climate, products, inhabitants, sports, animals, etc.

Main lesson (40 minutes)
* Give out the task sheets. Ask students to do Activity 1 in groups of four. Call back their ideas from the whole class. Also check that they have understood the vocabulary. Just accept the different suggestions you get, without commenting on their correctness.
* Give out/display the short short story 'The Bach' by Patricia Donnelly, and ask students to read it.
* Check with them how close their predictions had been.
* Ask students to do Activity 4 individually, then check with a partner. (Answers: (a) someone connected to the property developers who are taking over the island; (b) onto the island; (c) the Maoris'; (d) they are going to build a holiday centre – Pleasure Island; (e) an old lady; (f) a poor shack.)
* This activity concentrates students on the details of the bach itself. (Answers: (a) it was in bad condition, no pride or character; (b) a rusty horseshoe, shadowy furniture – of sorts, a heap of rags, a sagging bedframe, blackened frying pan, empty beer bottles, a handful of paperback romances, a spiral-bound notebook – the adjectives are all negative (rusty, shadow, sagging, blackened, empty); (c) dilapidated, dark, made from odds and ends – timber, driftwood, corrugated iron, salvage; (d) it was not well-constructed; (e) because *one man with a sledgehammer could bring the lot down*; (f) no electricity, water from a stream.)
* Activity 6 brings the students to the strange part of the story. (Answer: what is written in the book is the same as the start of the story; perhaps the old lady had magical or mystical powers, could see the future, maybe she was a Maori, to whom the land originally belonged . . . open to student interpretation.)

Plenary (10 minutes): Ask students to discuss their feelings about the story – is it spooky, ghostly, frightening, a horror story, a mystery, a chiller? It could be described as a circular story.

Homework: The writing task (Activity 8) asks students to analyse the structure of the story, to see how it works.

Differentiation: Students work on a story from a different culture.

TASK SHEET: **A hut and an old lady**

1. Look at these words and phrases:

landward end	*wharf*	*Maori owners*
time-share apartments	*dilapidated building*	*driftwood*
casino	*narrow strait*	

They all come from a short short story that you are going to read. Decide what each one means, and then work in a group of four to decide what you think the story might be about, and where it is set.

2. Now read the story 'The Bach'* by Patricia Donnelly.

3. How close were you predictions about the content of the story?

4. Answer these questions briefly:
    a) Who is the narrator?
    b) Where does he go?
    c) Whose land was it originally?
    d) What is going to happen there?
    e) Who was the last person to live there?
    f) What was the place she lived in like?
    Check your answers with a partner.

5. Look at the information you find about the bach.
    a) What is the significance of 'had been waiting such a long time that it had given up hope'?
    b) Make a list of the objects the narrator finds there. What do you notice about the adjectives which describe them?
    c) What was the building like? What was it made of?
    d) What does he mean when he says: 'All held together with cobwebs and dust'?
    e) Why does he say 'We wouldn't need the bulldozer'?
    f) What services did it have? Explain your answer.
    Check your answers with a partner.

6. What is strange about what is written in the notebook? What do you think about the old lady because of this?

7. How would you describe this kind of story? What genre is it? How does it make you feel?

8. There are ten paragraphs in this story. Write a description of how it is organized paragraph by paragraph.

[* *Bach* is a word used in New Zealand for a cottage, usually on a beach.]

Is there anybody there?

Introduction: This lesson uses a very famous mysterious poem that the students may have read before, but will probably not have analysed for form and content.

Aims and outcomes
- To read, enjoy and analyse a classic piece of English poetry
- To write a response to the poem

Resources required: The poem 'The Listeners' by Walter de la Mare, which is in many poetry anthologies, and can be found online at:

 www.poetry-archive.com/m/the_listeners.html
www.poetryfoundation.org/archive/poem.html?id=177007

Lesson starter (10 minutes): Write the word 'GHOST' on the board and elicit/provide some synonyms (e.g. spirit, spectre, phantom, wraith, poltergeist, spook). Ask if there is any difference between them (e.g. a poltergeist is supposed to make a lot of noise, moving things and knocking things over; spectre and wraith are rather archaic and literary).

Main lesson (40 minutes)
- Activity 1. Call back ideas from the whole class for general discussion.
- Students do Activity 3 quickly. (Answers: (a) a male traveller; (b) in a forest; (c) on a horse; (d) night; (e) phantom; (f) nothing; (g) left.)
- Activity 4. Vocabulary, some archaic. (Answers: (a) to eat noisily; (b) hit (from *smite*); (c) the ledge of the window, surrounded by the leaves of a creeper; (d) confused, not understanding; (e) a great many; (f) filling up with many together; (g) listening; (h) grazing; (i) old form of *spoke*; (j) place for the foot on a saddle; (k) moved with great force; (l) diving; (m) lived.)
- Activity 5. Elicit a range of suggestions from the class. (Possible answers: (a) to deliver a message, to collect something or someone; (b) the people who asked the Traveller to go there; (c) that he promised to do whatever it was; (d) everyone else in the vicinity is either asleep . . . dead.)
- Another activity asking for conjecture. (Possible answers: the Traveller rides off into the night; he feels annoyed at the wasted journey, afraid because 'they' will think he didn't do what he was supposed to, and might want revenge . . .)
- Activity 7 also asks for creative thinking. (Possible answers: the poem tells us they are *thronging the faint moonbeams on the dark stair* – so they are listening in the moonlight; they are the spirits of the people who lived in the house, the ghosts of the people he came to save . . .)
- Activity 8. Examining details. (Answers: *moonlit door; a bird flew out of the turret; leaf-fringed sill; he felt in his heart their strangeness/their stillness answering his cry.*)
- This activity asks for a formal analysis of the poem. (Answer: it is 36 lines long, with an ABCBDEFEGHIH . . . rhyme scheme throughout; line length varies from 6–13 syllables, with 7 syllables most frequent; all lines show initial capitalization, and enjambment is frequent.)

Plenary (10 minutes): Ask students for a summary of their ideas and feelings about the poem.

Homework: Students write a reply from the *phantom listeners* to the Traveller, saying what they would have said if they could speak. You may care to play them the YouTube video after they finish.

Differentiation: The poem allows for wide diversity of interpretation, and the homework task allows for an even wider range of possible answers.

TASK SHEET: **Is there anybody there?**

1. Work in a group of four. Pool your knowledge about ghosts – what they are, what they are supposed to do, whether they exist or not, etc.

2. Read the poem 'The Listeners' by Walter de la Mare.

3. Answer these questions quickly and briefly:
    a) Who is the protagonist?
    b) Where is the house?
    c) How did he get to the house?
    d) What time is it?
    e) What word is used for the ghosts?
    f) What did they say to the protagonist?
    g) What did the protagonist do in the end?
    Check your answers with a partner.

4. What do these words and phrases mean?
    a) *champed*
    b) *smote*
    c) *leaf-fringed sill*
    d) *perplexed*
    e) *host*
    f) *thronging*
    g) *hearkening*
    h) *cropping*
    i) *spake*
    l) *plunging*
    m) *dwelt*
    j) *stirrup*
    k) *surged*
    Check your answers with a partner.

5. Think about the actions and the people involved:
    a) Why did the Traveller go to the house in the first place?
    b) *Tell them I came* . . . Who are *them*?
    c) *I kept my word* . . . What does this imply?
    d) What do you understand by *the one man left awake* ?
    Discuss your ideas with a partner.

6. What is the result of what happens? How do you think the Traveller feels?

7. What are the *phantom listeners* like? What are they doing? Where are they? What do you think they are? Compare your ideas with a partner.

8. What elements in the poem create the spooky atmosphere?

9. Analyse the formal aspects of the poem.

10. The *phantom listeners* hear what the Traveller says, but they don't reply. Imagine that they wanted to reply to him but couldn't. Write what they wanted to tell him. You can do this as a poem or in prose.

A vivid imagination

Introduction: In this lesson students will work on a famous, classic short story by Saki, which is both a 'ghost' story and an amusing one.

Aims and outcomes

* To read, enjoy and analyse a classic short story

Resources required: The story 'The Open Window' from Saki (H. H. Munro) (1912) *Beasts and Super-beasts*, much anthologized; also found in H. H. Munro (1980) *The Complete Works of Saki*. London: The Bodley Head. It can be found online at:

 www.readbookonline.net/readOnLine/366

and you can hear it read very nicely by Roy Mcready at:

 www.youtube.com/watch?v=NhtcFpcmpzc

Lesson starter (10 minutes): Ask students what they understand by the term 'a tall story'. Elicit some examples, if possible, and/or tell one yourself.

Main lesson (40 minutes)

* Activity 1 aims to pre-teach some of the more unusual words and expressions found in the story. Give out the task sheet, and pair students to read the sentences and work out what they mean. They may need to use a dictionary. (Answers: (a) self-possessed = calm and organized; (b) without saying anything; (c) snipe = a kind of wading bird which is considered a game bird, too; (d) engulfed = completely covered; treacherous = unreliable; (e) faltered = started to break, become weak; (f) sympathetic comprehension = feeling sorry for and understanding their condition; (g) headlong retreat = they ran away quickly; (h) pariah dogs = feral dogs, dogs which have gone wild.)
* Hand out/display 'The Open Window' by Saki, down as far as 'Then she suddenly brightened into alert attention – but not to what Framton was saying' and ask students to read it.
* Activity 3 checks comprehension with true/false statements. Ask students to do it individually, then check with a partner. (Answers: (a) T; (b) F – they are waiting for Vera's aunt; (c) T; (d) T; (e) F – she comes from inside the house; (f) F – she says they all died in an accident in the bog; (g) F – she is bored by his talking about it; (h) F – she says it is the third anniversary of the men's accident.)
* Activity 4 asks students to make sure of their understanding of two key elements of the story. (Answers: (a) her husband, two brothers and their dog were drowned in the bog three years ago whilst out shooting; (b) because Mrs Sappleton still expects them to walk back in every day.)
* This shows Framton's feelings about the situation. (Answer: because Mrs Sappleton is talking as if the men will return any moment.)
* Activity 6 asks students to predict what will happen based on what has happened and the change in Mrs Sappleton. Elicit various suggestions from the whole class. (Answers: students' own predictions.)
* Hand out/display the second part of the story (from *'Here they are at last!'* to the end), and ask students to read it. Discuss whose ideas were closest to the original.
* Activity 8 asks them to understand Framton's behaviour. (Answer: he thought the three men were ghosts.)
* This asks students to understand Vera's behaviour throughout the story. (Answer: she makes

(continued on page 192)

TASK SHEET: **A vivid imagination**

1. Work with a partner and decide what these sentences mean:
   a) 'Do you like Sally?' 'She's OK, but she's too self-possessed for my taste.'
   b) He didn't seem to want to talk, so they sat there in silent communion.
   c) 'Did you go birdwatching yesterday?' 'Yes, but there wasn't much to see – just a few snipe in the marshes, as usual.'
   d) Oh, it was terrible! He was crossing the dry river bed, when he was engulfed by a sudden flood. It's such a treacherous river!
   e) She tried to sing it, but her voice faltered on the highest notes.
   f) Once he understood Paul's problem, he talked to him with sympathetic comprehension.
   g) When our reinforcements arrived, the enemy made a headlong retreat from the battlefield.
   h) If you walk in the Indian countryside, you must be careful of the packs of pariah dogs – they can have rabies.

2. Read the first part of the short story 'The Open Window' by Saki (H. H. Munro).

3. Say if these statements are true or false; correct any that are false.
   a) This scene takes place in a house in the country.
   b) Framton and Vera are waiting for Framton's sister.
   c) Vera tells Framton about her aunt's tragedy while they wait.
   d) Framton is there for a health cure.
   e) Mrs Sappleton comes in through the open window from the garden.
   f) Vera says Mrs Sappleton's husband killed her brother in a shooting accident.
   g) Mrs Sappleton is very interested in Framton's medical problems.
   h) Vera says that today is Mrs Sappleton's third wedding anniversary.
   Check your answers with a partner.

4. Explain to your partner in brief what Vera says about
   a) What happened to Mrs Sappleton's family.
   b) Why the window is open.

5. Mrs Sappleton comes in and starts talking. *To Framton, it was all purely* horrible. Why?

6. Read the last sentence of the first part again. Why do you think Mrs Sappleton suddenly changes? What do you think will happen next? Tell a partner.

7. Read the second part of the story. How did your prediction compare with what actually happened?

8. What did Framton do? Why?

9. How was Vera's reaction to Framton's disappearance similar to what she did on Framton's arrival? How does the final sentence reflect this?

10. Get into groups of seven (Vera, Framton, Mrs Sappleton, Mr Sappleton, the two brothers, and a narrator). Set up a space like the room in the story. The narrator reads the story, and the characters say what is in speech marks, and move appropriately.

11. How would you describe this story? What genre is it?

12. Write a summary of the story in 50 words.

up another tall story to explain Framton's sudden disappearance to her family. She was good at making up stories on the spot.)

- Group students as described, and have them 'perform' the story. Once they have worked out how to do it and practised a couple of times, have them perform it for others.

Plenary (10 minutes): Ask students to discuss Activity 11 as a whole class. (Answers: it's an amusing comedy story, with a ghostly element to it; it also shows much of Edwardian society.)

Homework: Students write a very short (50-word) summary of the story.

Differentiation: Students react to this story very differently depending on their own attitude to ghosts.

8.10 The dark day

Introduction: In this lesson, students invent their own 'strange story'.

Aims and outcomes

- To write a short short story about some strange event

Resources required: None.

Lesson starter (10 minutes): Write 'The Dark Day' on the board and brainstorm the ideas students come up with.

Main lesson (45 minutes)

- Hand out the task sheets, and ask students to work through Activity 1 immediately, bearing in mind the discussion you've just had. Emphasize that this is a *strange* story, and remind them of some of the *strange stories* they're read in this section – the normal turns strange (e.g. the bus-ride in 8.1), a person turns into an animal (8.3), strange behaviour by people (8.4, 8.5), something spooky (8.7, 8.8) or a trick tall story (8.9). (Note – if students find this difficult, you could ask them to write the story in pairs, rather than individually.)
- Ask students to decide on the two major problems they face on their 'dark day' and note them in the spaces in Activity 2.
- In Activities 3–4 they should plan the outline of their story into five paragraphs (4 and 6 are all right, too!) and decide when their two problems occur.

Plenary (5 minutes): Draw students' attention to the language examples in Activity 5, and suggest that they should use these in structuring their story through the paragraphs.

Homework (30 minutes in a subsequent lesson): Ask them to write the first draft of their story for homework.

- Next class, they should work with a partner, exchange writing and do a peer correction of each other's stories; explain that they should decide on the clarity and organization of the story, telling their partner where this breaks down. If, incidentally, they note any language problems (e.g. bad spelling, wrong tense used) they should underline that and leave their partner to work out what is wrong.
- They should then do a second draft and hand it in to you to read.

Differentiation: The open nature of this task allows all students to interpret it in their own way.

TASK SHEET: **The dark day**

1. You are going to write a *strange* story called 'The Dark Day'. Decide the following things, and note the details.
    a) Who are you? ....
    b) Where are you? ....
    c) Why is it dark? ....
    d) What are you going to do? ....
    e) Is there anyone else with you? ....

2. Choose two major problems that you face on this dark day:
    a) ....
    b) ....

3. Divide the story into five sections, and then work out what happens in each of them; decide when in these five periods of time the two major problems occur. Remember that it is a *strange* story, so anything can happen!

4. Plan the outline of your story using this framework:

Introduction (the information in 1)

....

Paragraph 1

....

Paragraph 2

....

Paragraph 3

....

Paragraph 4

....

Paragraph 5

....

Conclusion (How you get back to normal)

....

5. Make sure you sequence your story with the right discourse markers, for example: *first . . . then . . . next . . . after that . . . after some time . . . after a while . . . soon . . . later on . . . in the evening . . . finally . . . in the end . . .*

RESOURCE BANK: TEXTS FOR REFERENCE

SECTION 1: the World of School

1.3 Tensions at secondary school

From E.R. Braithwaite (1959) *To Sir, With Love*. Jove Books (Chapter 14, pages 107–109).

We pumped the ball hard, and while two of the boys held it firmly down on the table I laced it up tightly. In threading the thing through the last eyelet hole, however, the steel lace slipped and made a small wound on my finger, from which the blood slowly trickled.

"Blimey, red blood!"

Potter's large friendly face wore a look of simulated surprise, and the other boys burst into laughter at his goggle-eyed stare. Pamela moved quickly to Potter.

"What did you expect, fat boy? Ink?" she hissed at him; then calmly, disdainfully, she walked away to sit straight and aloof in her seat.

"Cor!" Denham gasped at the sheer venom of her attack.

Seales and Fernman merely stared from Potter to Pamela and back again, wordless with surprise. Poor Potter was flushed with embarrassment and stammered:

"I didn't mean anything, Sir; what I meant was, your colour is only skin deep."

I finished the lacing and opened the draw of my desk to find a strip of Elastoplast I kept there. I was annoyed with Pamela for the unnecessary and quite vehement attack on Potter, but I could think of nothing I could do about it without worsening an already delicate situation.

The boys walked over to Pamela, who observed their approach with cool unconcern.

"What's up with youse?" Denham planted himself squarely in front of her, and stuck his jaw forward belligerently.

"Are you addressing me, Denham?" "Yes." Pamela watched him and waited.

"All right, Miss Dare then. What's up with you?" "I don't know what you mean, Denham." She was cool, taunting.

"Pots was only being funny, and you had to go for him like that, and right in front of Sir. What did you want to call him 'fat boy' for?"

Pamela's gaze shifted from Denham to Potter and traversed him from top to toe.

"I was only having a little joke and Sir didn't mind," Potter offered, lamely, quailing under Pamela's examination.

At this, Pamela rose in one fierce, fluid motion. Eyes blazing, she stood straight before Potter and in her anger seemed to tower above him, her voice thick with emotion.

"Doesn't mind? How do you know he doesn't mind? Because he's decent about it and never lets on? Daft, that's what you are, the lot of youse, daft, stupid, soft!"

I sat down and watched, mesmerized by the concentrated anger of this red-headed Fury, who seemed to grow larger as she continued, her eyes boring into the helpless Potter.

"How would you like it if they were always on to you, fat Potter? Idiots, that what you are, idiots! My life, the silly things you ask!" She screwed up her face and fell into scathing mimicry:

"Do you ever wash, Sir? Do you feel the cold, Sir? Do you ever have a haircut, Sir? Stupid, that's what you are, all of youse." "Cor, good old Pamela!" exclaimed Tich Jackson.

Pamela swung around to fix him with her eyes, but Tich quickly altered it to:

"I mean, Miss Dare." "Sir said we could ask him anything we liked, didn't he?" persisted Denham. He was unable to match Pamela's quick cutting intelligence, but he stood firm, trying to cope with one idea at a time.

"You shut up, Denham. Call that asking questions, always on about his colour and that? Can't think of anything else to ask about?"

And as if unwilling to spare any of them she suddenly turned on Seales, who had, as usual, been playing the part of interested bystander.

"And you, you ought to know better." "Steady on, what have I done? I didn't say anything." He sounded rather alarmed.

"You never say anything. You're coloured too, but you sit back and keep your mouth shut. Are you scared of this lot?"

She was wonderful, tremendous in her scorn and towering anger: Boadicea revivified, flame-haired, majestic.

"I really don't think they meant any harm, Miss Dare. When they ask questions they're only trying to find out about things they don't understand."

Pamela was not to be mollified. "Then why don't they ask you if they're so keen to find out?" "I'm not Sir, Miss Dare, I only wish I was."

SECTION 2: The World of Work

2.2 The effects of work

From: Simon Armitage (1989) *Zoom!* Newcastle-upon-Tyne: Bloodaxe Books

Night Shift

Once again I have missed you by moments;
steam hugs the rim of the just-boiled kettle,

water in the pipes finds its own level.
In another room there are other signs

of someone having left: dust, unsettled
by the sweep of the curtains; the clockwork

contractions of the paraffin heater.
For weeks now we have come and gone, woken

in acres of empty bedding, written
lipstick love-notes on the bathroom mirror

and in this space we have worked and paid for
we have found ourselves, but lost each other.

Upstairs, at least, there is understanding in things
more telling than lipstick kisses:

the air, still hung with spores of your hairspray;
body-heat stowed in the crumpled duvet.

2.6 **Manufacturing biscuits**

From: Alain de Botton (2009) *The Pleasures and Sorrows of Work*. London: Hamish Hamilton.

Laurence led me to the boardroom where a table had been scattered with boxes of Moments, a six-centimetre-wide biscuit made of chocolate and shortcake, launched in the spring of 2006 at a ceremony (during which Laurence had made a speech in French) in a manufacturing plant in Belgium, following a two-year-long, £3 million development programme. Laurence was the biscuit's author.

This was not to say that Laurence knew how to bake, though he grew swiftly defensive in response to my expression of surprise at his inability. Biscuits are nowadays a branch of psychology, not cooking, he advised sternly.

Laurence had formulated his biscuit by gathering some interviewees in a hotel in Slough and, over a week, questioning them about their lives, in an attempt to tease out of them certain emotional longings that could subsequently be elaborated into the organizing principles behind a new product. In a conference room in the Thames Riviera hotel, a number of low-income mothers had spoken of their yearning for sympathy, affection and what Laurence termed simply, with aphoristic brevity, 'me-time'. The Moment set out to suggest itself as the plausible solution to their predicament.

The idea of answering psychological yearnings with dough might seem daunting. Laurence explained that in the hands of an experienced branding expert, decisions about width, shape, coating, packaging and name can furnish a biscuit with a personality as subtly and appropriately nuanced as that of a protagonist in a great novel.

Early on, it became evident to Laurence that his biscuit would need to be round rather than square, given the associations drawn in almost all cultures between the circle and femininity and wholeness. It was similarly imperative that it contain small pieces of raisin and whole chocolate chips to convey the impression of kindly indulgence – though because it was not outright decadence which was being evoked, no cream would be involved.

Laurence spent a further half a year working with colleagues on dilemmas of packaging, eventually resolving that a mere nine biscuits should be settled in a black plastic tray encased in a glossy twenty-four centimetre-long cardboard box. Laurence now initiated a debate about what to call the biscuits. Extensive consideration was given to Reflections, Retreats, Delights and, in a direct allusion to the biscuit's founding concept, My Times – before the right name came to Laurence in what could kindly be described as a flash of inspiration.

It was time for attention to be paid to the choice of fonts. The designers' initial layout had had the word Moments running in a romantic Edwardian script across the box, but there were concerns among some executives that this belied the product's projected function as a pleasant supplement to real life rather than a means of escape from it – an issue addressed by a last-minute change in the *m* and *s* to a more vertical orientation, as befitted a snack which respected the realities of life even as it offered temporary relief from them.

It is perhaps because many of us know what it is to spend an afternoon baking biscuits that there is something striking about encountering a company which relies on the labour of five thousand full-time employees to execute the task.

Manoeuvres which one might briefly have carried out on one's own in the kitchen (readying the oven, mixing the dough, writing a label) had at United Biscuits been isolated, codified and expanded to occupy entire working lives. Although all employment at the company was ultimately predicated on the sale of confectionery and salted snacks, a high percentage of the staff were, professionally speaking, many times removed from contact with anything one might eat. They were managing the forklift truck fleet in the warehouse or poring over the eighty or so words written along the sides of a typical packet of salted nuts. Some had attained extraordinary expertise in the collection and analysis of sales data from supermarkets, while others daily investigated how to ensure a minimum of friction between wafers during transit.

Along with such specialisation came a raft of esoteric job titles: Packaging Technologist, Branding Executive, Learning Centre Manager, Strategic Projects Evaluator. Careers ploughed deep and dedicated furrows: a start at Hula Hoops might be followed by promotion to Ridged Tortillas, a sideways shift to baked Mini Cheddars, a management role at McVite's Fruitsters and a swan-song post at Ginger Nuts.

3.4 Dinner time!

From Gerald Durrell (1972) *Catch Me A Colobus*. London: Collins.
In this extract, Gerald Durrell, then Director of the Jersey Wildlife Preservation Trust, is in Sierra Leone on a collecting expedition for his zoo.

It's one thing to look after an animal in a well conducted zoo where you have everything at your command, both from the feeding and the veterinary point of view, but it's a different kettle of fish when you are sitting five hundred miles from nowhere, with all your animals in little wooden boxes, and you have got to be everything from veterinary surgeon to maintenance man; and of course the animals, as soon as they have accepted captivity, start exhibiting all their eccentricities for your edification. It's curious the fads and fancies your animals develop. One day they'll go mad for oranges, for example, so you immediately increase your supply and shower oranges on them. The next day, if you give them an orange, they look at you as though you had mortally offended them and decide that they would much prefer peanuts. But unless you indulge them, as you would indulge an elderly lady with her pekinese, they will not be happy and they will not thrive.

We had, at one stage, a Scaly Anteater or Pangolin, brought in to us, which pleased me greatly because in the past, when I had collected in West Africa, I'd never had any success with these curious beasts that look like animated fir cones with tails. This was because they feed principally upon the ants that build their nests in trees, the ferocious little black tree ants. I had given the question of the pangolins' diet some thought while I was in England and had decided that, although they would take raw egg and milk and mincemeat as a mixture, something was obviously still lacking, and that something must be a trace of formic acid. So on this occasion I had brought a small bottle of formic acid out with me in order to try it, and I made up the mixture for the pangolin every day. I often wondered, as I was doing this, how a TV cook would describe this recipe:

Take two tablespoonfuls of powdered milk, darlings; beat it up into a quarter of a pint of water, and when this is of a smooth creamy consistency, add one raw egg and beat it briskly until it is thoroughly mixed. Then place into this a handful of finely minced raw meat; stir gently, and finally garnish with a small portion of chopped tree ants' nest and a drop of formic acid. Serve immediately. You will be delighted with the effect that this recipe will have on your guests, and will, without doubt, be the most popular pangolin party thrower of the season.

It would, I reflected, be interesting to do a sort of cookery book for the animal collectors; a kind of *Larousse Gastronomique* dealing with the best ways of serving maggots and so on.

3.5 One for Sorrow

From: Esther Morgan (2001) *Beyond Calling Distance*. Tarset: Bloodaxe Books.

Magpie

A crow –
but mobster-style –
shoe-shine black
spats white.
A flash character
dressed for dinner
on the hard shoulder.
Egg-filcher – the yolk
sliding easy down
your glossy throat.
You jab the hole
through the gold top,
suck the cream out.

A sharp eye
for glitter in the grass.
Dream-hoarder –
lining your nest
with silver foil,
bits of coloured glass,
diamanté, paste,
every single earring
I've ever lost.
You'd nick the ring
from my dead mum's finger,
the words right out
of our gaping mouths.

A loner at heart
I meet you
strutting in the road,
dipping your sticky
black beak.
You make me slow
down, almost stop –
a lazy hopping flap
at the last moment.
You eye me up
as I drive past.
Bad luck.
I salute you.

SECTION 4: Family

4.1 A Sister

From: J. C. Hall (1985) *Selected and New Poems: 1939–84.* London: Secker & Warburg.

Little sister

Until I was nine we shared a room,
Little sister, you and I in the dark,
My shirt folded beside your dress.
Often, halfwaking, you sought my arm,
Your breath calming against my cheek
After some dream distress.

Morning was boy-time, you also
Clambering rocks, spotting trains,
The stream twirling our boats.
Evening softened to fire-glow,
Encyclopaedias, guess games,
The piano stumbling over its notes.

Later such comradeship was thought unwise.
I slept alone, went to a different school
(More like a foreign land!).
Growing-up was growing apart. New girls had ways
Smarter than yours, you brought home real
Boyfriends I couldn't stand,

Married a brotherly sort of chap
And had a boy, a girl, and so
Started that round again. A snap (I think it's you) nicely suggests
A woman men like to know,
Gentle and serious yet full of zest.

I greet you there, a shimmering she
On the far side of my mind, a love
Softly focused, never outworn.
I have made this history
Out of a life life couldn't achieve,
Little sister – you who were never born.

Mother and Daughter

From: Anne Haverty (1999) *The Beauty of the Moon*. London: Chatto & Windus.

Mother and Daughter in Bewley's Café

Farther and farther they go into silence,
Eat their grill and then their gateaux
Knowing how to do this together.

There's something alike.
A look about the mouth that will
Fold with time in the same way,
Hair that may only have faded from
How the younger's is. But really,
You could never tell.

The mother, appalled
At the unfair passage of the years,
Gazes sullen as an adolescent.
In carriers around her feet,
New clothes for winter no-one
Will notice. Except her sister
Who'll ask first how much.

Nothing to say, they nurse
Their secrets. Dreams
Of deceit, of love, of glory.
An unfilial future. A makeshift past.

Idly, Girl spoons the sugar,
Applauds Mother's empty plate
And, splendid eyes downcast, frankly
Unreins her filly's mane for a boy
In the corner bored with his tea.
Mother sees what her mam saw –
No sooner here than gone.

4.6 An Unknown Aunt

From: Matthew Sweeney (1992) *Cacti*. London: Secker and Warburg.

The Aunt I Never Met

The aunt I never met was black-haired
and holy. She sang in the choir
on Sundays. She also helped
my grandfather butcher the lambs
he kept in the long grass at the back –
even he agreed she was the best
with the cleaver. She played tennis
with priests, and beat them,
and drank Bloody Marys from a bottle
during whist drives, and owned
the only yellow bubblecar in Ulster
(now in private collection
in Guersney). During the war
she took up German, crossed her sevens,
lit the odd bonfire at night
on the cliff edge, and did no good.
French toast and salmon were her favourites.
She hated kids – her eventual undoing,
if you ask me. Why else did she
end her days in that old farmhouse
hidden by trees, where the outside light
stayed on all night to lure
Visitors, even family, who never came?
Why else did I never meet her?

From: Edward Storey (1969) *North Bank Night*. London: Chatto & Windus.

In Memory of My Grandfather

Swearing about the weather he walked in
like an old tree and sat down;
his beard charred with tobacco, his voice
rough as the bark of his cracked hands.

Whenever he came it was the wrong time.
Roots spread over the hearth, tripped
whoever tried to move about the room –
the house was cramped with only furniture.

But I was glad of his coming. Only
through him could I breathe in the sun
and the smell of fields. His clothes reeked
of the soil and the world outside;

Geese and cows were the colour he made them,
he knew the language of birds and brought them
singing out of his beard, alive
to my blankets. He was winter and harvest.

Plums shone in his eyes when he rambled
of orchards. With giant thumbs he'd split
an apple through the core, and juice
flowed from his ripe, uncultured mouth.

Then, hearing the room clock chime,
he walked from my ceiling of farmyards
and returned to his forest of thunder.
The house regained silence and corners.

Slumped there in my summerless season
I longed for his rough hands and words
to break the restrictions of my bed,
to burst like a tree from my four walls.

But there was no chance again of miming
his habits or language. Only now,
years later in a cramped city, can I
be grateful for his influence and love.

5.2 Traditional Indian cookery

From: Anjum Anand (2003) *Indian Every Day*. London: Headline Book Publishing.

Spice Up Your Health

The ancient wisdom of Ayurveda (meaning knowledge of how to live) has been guiding the population of India on how to maintain optimum health for over five thousand years. Our bodies are delicately balanced systems and small external changes or stresses disturb our natural equilibrium. Ayurveda practitioners prescribe appropriate diets, natural medicines and lots of rest to cure these imbalances.

Following an Ayurvedic diet (which is an eating plan rather than systematic deprivation) means enjoying a variety of freshly cooked meals, with a balance of flavours and nutrients. The general rules are:

- All meals should supply the body with carbohydrates, protein and a little fat.
- Restrict meats and alcohol.
- Avoid additives and preservatives.
- Limit your intake of raw vegetables as they are considered difficult to digest.
- Stick to whole grains rather than refined products.
- Meals should be freshly prepared and hot to aid digestion.
- You should only sit down to a meal once the last one has been digested.
- The food type should suit the time of year with more sweet and sour food being eaten in winter (that is, more carbohydrates and fats).
- Focus on your meal as you eat, maintain an even pace and stop when you are full.
- Lastly, for all the vibration-sensitive people out there, the food should be prepared lovingly and eaten in a relaxing atmosphere.

Most of this advice will sound familiar and is good common sense. This may seem excessive, but a look at the ingredients listed on the packet of any convenience meal will show just how many things go into it. I know most of us don't have the time to think about what to eat, let alone cook it, but the positive effects of doing so will last longer than a session at the gym or an evening in the pub.

Indian meals traditionally contain a spectrum of ingredients spanning the food groups. The building blocks of Indian cuisine are now accepted as being highly beneficial for health and are revered for their preventative and curative powers. The main super-ingredients are tomatoes, onions, garlic, ginger, yoghurt and spices. In fact, spices are considered to be the *crème de la crème*, possessing powerful antibacterial and antioxidant properties. Indian sages discovered and understood these benefits centuries ago and carefully wove them into the fabric of our cuisine.

From: Rose Tremain (2007) *The Road Home*. London: Vintage.

In this scene, the Chef, GK Ashe, has just welcomed Polish migrant Lev (whom he calls 'nurse' and 'Olev'), to his kitchen team, as washer-up.

GK smiled. He pirouetted away from Lev, but turned to say: 'New menu begins this evening, so it may get a bit hot in here, there may be a fair bit of replating going on, but what do nurses do? They stay calm. They clear up the mess. You got it? We're counting on you, Olev.'

More staff began to arrive. They came over and introduced themselves to Lev, and Lev tried to remember their names: Tony and Pierre, the sous-chefs; Waldo, pâtisserie and pudding chef; Sophie, vegetable and salad preparation; then the waiters, Stuart, Jeb and Mario. All were yonger than Lev and seemed solemn, as actors seem when they're nervous.

At five, the group sat down at a table at the back of the restaurant and Jeb served poached chicken legs with celery, carrots and *gnocchi*, cooked by Tony. Lev ate very slowly. There was some cleansing herb in the *gnocchi* he wanted to identify. He savoured the delicious potato ball, rolled it round his mouth. Parsley, that was it. He ate it silently, wondering how it was made, while all around him the dishes for the new menu were being discussed and final notes scribbled by the chefs.

'Plating up the trout terrine,' he heard GK Ashe say, 'I want the leaves in a rosette-shape and clear of the slice. I don't want them touching the fish or lying all over the plate like some stupid paperchase. Barely dress them, OK? Just a glisten of vinaigrette. And the grapefruit mayonnaise should look like an army button on the cuff of the terrine. You see the image?' 'Yes, Chef,' said Pierre.

'And keep mit small,' GK went on. 'The trout's moist enough, rich enough. What we're saying with this mayo is, OK, we're going to spoil you now, but not too much. You have to *savour* it.'

Lev understood only words here and there. He ate more *gnocchi*. He imagined serving these, in their beautiful chicken broth, to Maya.

The menu discussion went on, charged with intensity. 'The *pintade*, Chef,' said Tony. 'The *vin de noix* is going to make it lovely and dark. I was thinking . . . lay on the breast three batons of . . . maybe steamed beetroot, and get a nice vibrant colour contrast.' 'No,' said Ashe. 'No beetroot. *Cèpes*. We discussed this. Just the *cèpes* and a little sandcastle of potato gratin. Now, everybody OK with the halibut?' 'Yes, Chef.' 'Did you get some nice endive, Pierre?' 'Yes, Chef.' 'Don't overcook it, then. I don't want to see my lovely halibut sitting on bogie-slime.' 'There was a clatter of laughter. Sophie said: 'You're putting me off my grub, Chef.' 'Good,' said GK. 'You're too fat as it is.'

The group went silent. Lev looked up and saw Sophie blush and lay down her knife and fork on her half-finished meal, and he remembered Lora once saying: 'In a workplace, as a woman in this country, you're fighting a war. Every day.'

He looked away from Sophie as Stuart and Mario cleared away the chicken plates and Waldo brought in a dish of *crème brûlée*, its crust still bubbling from his blow-torch.

'Chef,' said Waldo. 'I want everybody to try this. I'm using blueberries, just cooked for one minute to soften their shape, as a nice astringent base to the *crème*.' 'OK,' said GK. 'Give us a spoon.' Then he turned to Lev. 'You taste this too,' he said. 'We call desserts "puddings" in England; hangover from the days when that's what desserts were: steamed puddings. It's probably why Queen Victoria was the shape she was. But in Britain now a pudding can be a mint sorbet; it can be a poached lychee in a spun-sugar basket. You get it, Olev?' 'Pudding?' said Lev. 'Yes. I know English pudding.' 'Sure,' said GK, lightly investigating the *brûlée* crust with the edge of his spoon. 'but now you can know it properly – know it for what it means. If you're coming to work in a kitchen, Olev, you have to get the words right. You have to get the *glossary* into your head.' 'I will Chef,' said Lev. And he wanted to add, as politely as he could, that there was one word G. K. Ashe could get into his head and that word was 'Lev', but when he opened his mouth to speak, GK had turned away and was concentrating on Waldo's *brûlée*.

'I like it, said Damian. 'It's quite refreshing.' 'Bloody nice, Waldo,' said Mario.

'It's OK,' said GK, 'but vary the fruit base over the week. Try rhubarb. Try damsons.'

5.5 Making rice pudding

From: Michael Laskey (1999) *The Tightrope Wedding*. Huddersfield: Smith/Doorstop Books.

Pudding

For years she tried to get it right,
off and on. No cinnamon,
she learnt, and less vanilla essence.
A pinch of nutmeg, half an ounce
more sugar than it said, not brown –
as she'd used once – but caster.

It was his favourite, so she made it
often and achieved such moistness
in the middle and a skin
so delicate and thickly freckled
he was baffled, just couldn't say
the way his mum's had differed.

At last she'd asked her – it was after
Olga died, when all that sadness
softened them – and she admitted
that what she did was add a little
tin of Ambrosia Creamed Rice.
It's been fresh fruit ever since.

Eating sushi at home

From: Tobias Hill (1998) *Zoo*. Oxford: Oxford University Press.

Sushi

In the small hours
we eat sushi with our fingers.
It is a cold night
outside, and traffic
lights up the ceiling

in passing. On your skin
is the smell
of sweet abalone,
sweat, and ark shell, and bluefin.

You are picking
red salmon eggs
from white rice
carefully,
like a child with a chocolate biscuit.

On your palms
you warm the eggs,
their soft red pearls.

You break them open –
their skins are so tender –
with the tip of your tongue.

It is a warm night
and my heart is skipping
along, skipping along –

I would kiss you,
but this is a time to remember
and first I will watch you
eating, and your grin
quick in the dark. I'm getting it clear,

so when I cast my mind back here
it will come skipping,
like a flat stone across flat water.

SECTION 6: On the Road

6.1 **Walking to the Danube**

From: Philip Ó Ceallaigh 'Walking to the Danube' in (2006) *Notes from a Turkish Whorehouse*. Dublin: Penguin Ireland.

Walking to the Danube

I

It was evening and I was walking between rows of poplars down a gravel road that rose and fell gently, the low sun coming in hard shafts between breaks in bruised clouds. The fields were shades of yellow – corn and wheat and grass – and in the distance were the black hills. I was walking to the Danube, forty kilometres south. I was alone and my feet were moving and the landscape was moving and I felt well enough. But I had no water and had to think about a place to camp.

I came to a well. I lowered the bucket down and as I raised it all the water spilled through the holes. By my third try I was able to raise it fast enough and drink from the metal cup chained to the well. Then, walking behind a hay cart, I entered the village.

Ilidia was one long cobbled street fronted by a row of solid houses. I had time to make the next village, but an old woman I asked directions from told me I could pass the night at her place. I entered the courtyard expecting to pitch my tent behind the house, and then I was in her house, her grandchildren preparing me a room. Andrea, twelve years old, talking very quickly as she made up the bed, was sharp and curious. Her sister, a year older, blonde and plump, watched us, giggling.

The girls showed me the village as it grew dark. They were at home in their place, proud of their animals and fruit trees and streets. Adults learn to be ashamed. They learn that they are poor, that the place they live in has been left behind. One little girl remembered me. She said she had been on the hay cart when I entered the village. She pointed at the stream and told me she was afraid because once she had seen a snake in the water.

Inside, night fallen, the grandmother gave me bread and onion and home-made cheese and butter and warm milk. The grandfather asked if I did not mind travelling alone. He asked why I was walking. Was I not afraid of wild animals? Then he said:

'The Swiss do a lot of work with gold.'

I nodded. I did not know what to say.

Andrea showed me photographs. Grandad had always had that blank look. He was good for cutting hay. Grandmother held things together. There were pictures of a man: 'Father, who left us.' In the wedding photographs Father had a vague, unfocused expression. A man who likes a good time. The bride, big eighties hair, plain and apprehensive, due to be abandoned. It is all very clear afterwards, in a snap. There was a photo of the couple outside the Miners' Restaurant, where the reception was held. It all happened in the nearby mining town of Anina, now depressed as the industry collapses. In the summer, Andrea told me, she and her sister went back to the grandparents and the village.

There was no toilet and I was shown the backyard. It was a starry night. The goats watched me with their green demonic eyes.

In the inner courtyard the old woman was drawing water and I asked her what I owed. But she did not want my money. She wanted me to thank God, and for the girls to grow up well.

In the morning she fried me an egg. It was the feast of Saint Ilie, the patron of the village, and nobody would be working. She had been good to me and I felt like acting holy to please her, so I went down with Andrea to look at the village church. When I went she pressed a bottle of milk and cheese and peppers on me. I was accumulating food; the day before, the grandparents of friends had given me cheese and peppers and a big slab of *slanina*, salted pork fat.

So, down the dirt road to Socolari, where there was only one shop, then to Potoc, even more remote and straggling. There was no shop in Potoc and many of the houses were abandoned. It was a dying place. The only people left were old. Then I was in open country, and heading upriver along the banks of the Nera. In the early afternoon the weather turned bad and I pitched the tent for the first time.

6.5 In olden days

From: Giuseppe di Lampedusa (1958; trans 1960) *The Leopard*. London: Flamingo.

From: Chapter 2: Donnafugata (intact, except for one three-line omission of unnecessary tangential detail).

In this scene the Prince Salina and his family and entourage are travelling south from their home near Palermo to Donnafugata.

'The trees! The trees!'

This shout from the leading carriage eddied back along the following four, almost invisible in clouds of white dust; and at every window perspiring faces expressed tired gratification.

The trees were only three, in truth, and eucalyptus at that, the scruffiest of Mother Nature's children. But they were also the first seen by the Salina family since leaving Bisacquino at six that morning. It was now eleven, and for the last five hours all they had set eyes on were bare hillsides flaming yellow under the sun. Trots over level ground had alternated briefly with long slow trudges uphill and then careful shuffles down; both trudge and trot merging, anyway, into the constant jingle of harness bells, imperceptible now to the dazed senses except as sound equivalent of the blazing landscape. They had passed through crazed-looking villages washed in the palest blue; crossed dry beds of torrents over fantastic bridges; skirted sheer precipices which no sage and broom could temper. Never a tree, never a drop of water; just sun and dust. Inside the carriages, tight shut against that sun and dust, the temperature must have been well over 120 degrees. Those desiccated trees yearning away under bleached sky bore many a message; that they were now within a couple of hours from their journey's end; that they were entering family estates; that they could lunch, and perhaps even wash their faces in the verminous waters of the well.

Ten minutes later they reached the farm buildings of Rampinzeri; a huge pile, only used one month in the year by labourers, mules and cattle gathered there for the harvest. Over the great yet staved-in door a stone Leopard pranced in spite of legs broken off by flung stones; next to the main farm building a deep well, watched over by those eucalyptuses, mutely offered various services: as swimming pool, drinking trough, prison or cemetery. It slaked thirst, spread typhus, guarded the kidnapped and hid the corpses both of animals and men till they were reduced to the smoothest of anonymous skeletons.

The whole Salina family alighted from their various carriages. The Prince cheered by the thought of soon reaching his beloved Donnafugata, the Princess irritated and yet inert, part restored, however, by her husband's serenity; tired girls; boys excited by novelty and untamed by the heat; Mademoiselle Dombreuil, the French governess, utterly exhausted, remembering years spent in Algeria with the family of Marshal Bugeaud, moaning '*Mon Dieu, mon Dieu, c'est pire qu'en Afrique!*' and mopping at her turned-up nose; Father Pirrone, whose breviary-reading had lulled him into a sleep which had shortened the whole trip and made him the spryest of the party; a maid and two lackeys, city folk worried by the unusual aspect of the countryside; and Bendicò, who had rushed out of the last carriage and was baying at the funereal suggestions of rooks swirling low in the light.

All were white with dust to the eyebrows, lips or pigtails; whitish puffs arose around those who had reached the stopping-place and were dusting each other down.

Amid this dirt Tancredi's elegant spruceness stood out all the more. He had travelled on horseback and, reaching the farm half an hour before the carriages, had time to shake off dust, brush up and change his white cravat. While drawing some water from the well of many uses he had glanced for a second into the mirror of the bucket and found himself in good order. He helped the Prince to alight, dusted the Prince's top hat with his sleeve, distributed sweets to his girl cousins and quips to the boys, almost genuflected before the Jesuit, returned the passionate hugs of Bendicò, consoled Mademoiselle Dombreuil, laughed at all, enchanted all.

The coachmen were walking the horses slowly round to freshen them up before watering, the lackeys laying the table-cloths out on straw left over from the threshing, in the oblong shade from the building. Luncheon began near the accommodating well. All around quivered the funereal countryside, yellow with stubble, black with burnt patches; the lament of cicadas filled the sky. It was like a death-rattle from parched Sicily at the end of August vainly awaiting rain.

SECTION 7: Places

7.2 **In a Welsh slate mine**

From: Gillian Clarke (1989) *Letting in the Rumour*. Manchester: Carcanet.

Slate Mine

Into the dark out of June heat,
under the forest's root, past Private,
Danger, Forbidden, past wheels, pulleys,
chains stilled in the pollens of rust.

We stoop through its porch,
to the knees in ice. Torchlight flutters
on wet stone and dies at the brink
of the first gallery.

In the next, and the next, emptiness deep
as cathedrals, then one where a stream hangs
three hundred feet in glittering stillness
and ferns lean to drink at sunlight.

Rungs crook rusted fingers over the drop,
the miner's footprint in air, his hand-print
on rockface and roofscape slimed
by a century of rain.

My cast slate panics
through generations of silence,
such a long wait
for the sound of drowning.

7.4 A rococo room

The Inheritance

From: Magda Szabó (1987; trans 2005) *The Door*. London: Vintage.
Translated by Len Rix.
The narrator has come with an official to look at what she has been left by a lady called Emerence.

We stepped in together. It was pitch black inside and at first we could make nothing out. Of course – the shutters. The Lieutenant Colonel felt along the wall. Near the door, some of the disinfectant smell had seeped through, the place hadn't been aired for God knows how long, and we began to cough in the choking fumes. Finally he located the switch. The instant the light came on he thrust me back into the outer room, the one now fully restored to order. He'd glimpsed me struggling with nausea, as if poisoned by gas. Only when he'd thrown every window open did he let me back in. But I'd already seen all I needed of Emerence's bequest.

You see this kind of thing in films, but even then the eye has difficulty believing. Dust inches deep covers the furniture; spider's webs fly into the actors' faces and hair with every move they make. If she had once protected her things with sheets, they must have been taken off immediately after the police inspection, because they were nowhere to be seen. I stood in the most beautifully furnished room I had ever seen. I brushed the side of my hand along one of the armchairs, and a pale-pink velvet glowed in its gilded rococo frame. I was standing in a salon of the late-eighteenth-century, a museum treasure, the *chef d'oeuvre* of some craftsman who supplied the aristocracy. For the house I had never bought I now possessed a drawing-room table with porcelain inlays on which shepherds chased after lambs, and a little couch with tiny gilded legs as slender as those of a young kitten. As I patted the upholstery the dust billowed up and then drifted down again. But the blow had split the fabric, which tore as if killed by unkindness. A console mirror rose all the way to the ceiling. On a small table stood two porcelain figurines, and, between then, something at last alive, a perpetual clock, showing the days, the phases of the moon and revolutions of the stars. It was still working. I went to dust it off, but the Lieutenant Colonel stopped me.

"Don't touch anything," he warned. "It's dangerous to move anything. The covers have perished, the furniture's dead. Everything here is dead, except the clock. Let me lift it down."

I wanted to take the figurines in my hands, or look to see what, if anything, there was in the console, and I didn't listen. I grasped the handle of a drawer. It didn't respond. I would have to play with it, to learn the special secret movement to which it would yield, which only the family would have known. What followed was very different. Suddenly everything around me became a vision out of Kafka, or a horror film: the console collapsed. Not with brutal swiftness but gently, gradually, it began to disintegrate into a river of golden sawdust. The figurines tumbled down, along with the clock. The frame of the console and its table crumbled into nothing; the drawers and legs were no more than dust.

"Woodworm," the Lieutenant Colonel said. "You won't be able to take anything from here. It's all finished. Emerence hasn't opened the door since she let me in for the inspection. So, this was her reward for saving Eva Grossman. As it was, it would have been worth a fortune, but you can see it's ruined. Look."

He pressed the palm of his hand into an armchair and it too collapsed. The chairs went down, the velvet splitting into strips and bursting from the wooden frames. The legs were turning to powder before our eyes, as if some secret chemical preparation had kept them alive only so long as they remained unseen by human eye.

"There's nothing here you could use," the Lieutenant Colonel said. "I'll have it cleared away. Will you take the clock? It's still ticking. The figurines, I'm sorry to say, were broken."

I didn't want the clock. It stayed on the floor. I didn't want anything. I didn't even look back – that's how I left Emerence's home, still incapable of tears. The Lieutenant Colonel took his leave, but didn't bother to shut the door behind him. Adélka told me that when the team of cleaners arrived and looked in, neither the shattered porcelain nor the clock were there. There was nothing, only the pulverized furniture. But I was no longer interested.

SECTION 8: Strange Stories

8.1 Catching a bus

From: Neil Rollinson (1996) *A Spillage of Mercury*. London: Cape Poetry.

The Last Bus To Nowhere

As I came round the corner
the bus was just leaving. It was
hot, and I wasn't in a rush,
but something snapped in my head
and I started to run.
As it pulled away and picked up speed
I was full tilt in its slipstream.
White lines flashed below,
sweat bubbled under my hair.
The bus crunched into second gear
as I was moving smoothly
into third, breathing pure diesl,
the trees in the park
flickered by like Super-8 film:
a child hung motionless in a swing.
After fifty metres it was touch and go,
but I'd got to the point of no return,
my legs were sheer motion, I could
see the faces of startled drivers
in the opposite lane.
As the bus lurched into third
I managed to get my hands
on the pole at the back,
but when I jumped, my legs flailed,
I could feel my toe caps
scraping the tarmac.
I clung on tight,
trailing behind
like an earthing-strip,
a diver in mid belly-flop.
The inside of the bus was as calm
as somebody's sitting room, people
were reading the morning papers, listening
to walkmans. I felt weak, the road
rushed under me like rapids,
and with a last almighty effort
I pulled with my arms, got my knees
onto the platform, crawled
on all fours to the first seat in the bus,
and sat there trembling, trying
to sort the change in my pocket.

A short short story by Patricia Donnelly in Graeme Lay (Ed.) (1997) *100 NZ short short stories*. New Zealand, North Shore City: Tandem Press.

The Bach

The old cottage sat in a heap on the beach, just by the landward end of the wharf. It looked as if it was waiting for the next boat out – had been waiting for such a long time that it had given up hope.

The island had passed through a variety of hands since last century, when its Maori owners had, by all accounts, been judicially robbed. No doubt it was due to feature in some future land claim, but that would be somebody else's worry.

My job was to see that everything was ready for the developers to move in. That would mean bulldozers, barged across the narrow strait on a calm day. The two or three modern holiday homes, mostly on the far side of the island, could stay. They'd have company soon, and lots of it, with time-share apartments, a caravan camp and, it was hoped, a casino. Pleasure Island, the brochures were calling it.

The wharf was sound enough, and there was a metalled track that ran inland, past the dilapidated building. I paused at the sagging door with its rusty horseshoe – all the luck ran out of it. The old man had told me, last night in the pub on the mainland, that the bach had been used as a builders' hut from time to time. The gangs would stay there, weeks on end, augmenting their diet of tinned food with fresh oysters from the rocks.

Nobody lives there now, he said. But there used to be an old girl – not that I ever saw her myself. Went across when the ferry was still running and missed the last one back, so they say.

Even with the doors left open, the interior was dark. Shadowy furniture – of sorts – still waited for the next occupant. Like the building itself, it was made from odds and ends – timber, driftwood, corrugated iron. Things the builders hadn't needed, even salvaged from the occasional shipwreck from the look of it. All held together with cobwebs and dust. We wouldn't need the bulldozer, I thought – one man with a sledgehammer could bring the whole lot down.

Just the one room. A heap of rags on a sagging bedframe in one corner served as sleeping quarters. No electricity. A nearby stream supplied all the usual conveniences.

Blackened frypan, empty beer bottles, and on the shelf beside them, a handful of paperback books. Romances, most of them. The story about the old girl squatting here must be true, then. I wondered where she'd gone.

A spiral-bound notebook caught my eye. Picking it up, I tried to decipher the pencil scrawl. Now and again the odd word would stand out, making me curiously uneasy.

Then, returning to the first page, I read: *The old cottage sat in a heap on the beach, just by the landward end of the wharf. It looked as if it was waiting for the next boat out.*